WHO DO I THINK I AM?

WHO DO I THINK I AM?

Exploring personal identity and what it
means to be "in Christ"

David Claydon

Morling Press

Morling Press
First Published 2013
120 Herring Rd Macquarie Park NSW 2113 Australia
Phone: +61 2 9878 0201
Email: enquiries@morling.edu.au
www.morlingcollege.com

© **Morling Press 2013**

The publication is copyright. Other than for the purposes of study and subject to the conditions of the Copyright Act, no part of it in any form or by any means (electronic, mechanical, micro-copying, photocopying or otherwise) may be reproduced, stored in a retrieval system or transmitted without the permission of the publisher.

Scripture quotations are from The Holy Bible, English Standard Version® (ESV®), copyright© 2001 by Crossway Bibles, a publishing ministry of Good News Publishers. Used by permission. All rights reserved.

ISBN: 978-0-9806421-9-3

Designed by Morling Press **www.morlingcollege.com/morlingpress**

To my wife Robyn for her constant support and encouragement, our daughter Kim and her husband David, our grandchildren Andrew and Georgia and my sister-in-law Marlene — all of whom have contributed in significant ways to the shaping of my identity.

Chapters

Acknowledgments 9
1. Who Am I? 11
2. Do I Really Matter? 15
3. In God's Image but Not Divine 22
4. What Are the Characteristics of Being Made in God's Image? 29
5. The Beauty of Relationships 37
6. Self-Esteem and How Others See Me 45
7. Identity Has Continuity 52
8. The Social Self 59
9. Our Soul, Spirit and Body 66
10. If I Think I Am a Failure 76
11. God's Identity 80
12. Being in Christ — Part I 86
13. Being in Christ — Part II 94
14. What Makes Us What We Are Now? 99
15. The Emerging Identity through the Growing Years 106
16. My Humility and Identity 113
17. National and Community Identities 119
18. Identities Determined by Religion 124
19. Ethnic Identity and the Missionary Challenge 134
20. The Identity of the Church and Personal Connections 139
21. A Final Word 145
Bibliography 146

Acknowledgments

I express appreciation to Dr W.E. Andersen AM for his insightful suggestions and to my grandson, Andrew Barker, for helpful editorial comments.

Chapter 1

Who Am I?

Growing up on my own — no parents!

Most people know their date of birth and the names of their parents. I am, however, ignorant on both counts! When I have to put "parents' names" on a document, I usually put N/A (not applicable) much to the amusement of my grandchildren and the confusion of those looking at the document! It might seem that I can handle this potentially difficult situation with a degree of good humour, but it was not always so.

To answer the question "who am I?" is not easy when you are uncertain about your origins, or are confused about which culture you belong to.

This book examines the question of identity and much of my thinking has been influenced by the different cultures in which I have lived and what I remember of the early years of my life.

I was born in Bethlehem, the son of an English couple who were in the Middle East with the British Mandate Government. The British Mandate controlled Palestine after the First World War, which until then was included in the Ottoman Empire (based in Turkey). The Ottoman Empire was linked to Germany in the war and so lost control when the war was lost. Another aspect of the British Mandate was to allow Zionists from Europe to migrate to Palestine and settle down there. There was fighting between the Zionists and the Palestinians. The British Mandate leaders were caught up in this fighting and my parents were among those killed. I was just a few months old and having no other relative in Palestine, was placed in an orphanage. Here I stayed for four years, a red-headed English boy among dozens of Arabic orphans. Consequently my first language was Arabic, a language I wish I still retained.

In 1941, with the Second World War well under way, I was about four and because the matron was a German she was interned and the orphanage closed. Lora, an Australian, who had previously been working as a missionary in India, came to Jerusalem as a social worker and one of her first assignments was to find a home for all the orphans. She had little difficulty in finding extended families for the Arabic children, but what to do with a little English boy was more of a challenge! At the time the orphanage was in the process of being closed, I, and most of the children, contracted measles and we were put into the German hospital. This hospital had to be closed as all the staff were also to be interned. The Palestinian children were eventually taken to be with extended families and I was left. Lora, the social worker, gathered me up in a blanket and took me to a Christian hospital.

Years later, when my biography and that of my wife was being written, the author asked what the book should be called. I replied, "Call it *Never Alone*" because, although through most of my growing-up years I was, from a human point of view, alone, I always felt that I was never completely alone as Jesus was with me. It was while I was in the Christian hospital that something happened which made me realise that God loved me and was always there for me. On the wall was a picture of Jesus with a lamb and an inscription, "The Good Shepherd". A visiting teacher told us the story of Jesus' care for the sheep that was lost and I remember thinking "if Jesus could care for a lost lamb, he could care for a lost boy". This was a great comfort to me and, as I look back, was a significant part of my growing sense of identity. I belonged — not to parents or family — but to Jesus.

I remained in Palestine until I was eight, living the latter years with an English family in a Jewish compound. We coped with the air raids of WWII and the local bombings of our own triangle war between the Mandate Government, the Palestinians and the Zionists. War, to a small boy, was an everyday occurrence and I don't remember being frightened.

A positive self-image

One positive experience was when Lora was appointed as a translator (in Hindi and Urdu) for the English doctors who ran the war hospital at Lod Airport in Palestine for wounded Indian Army soldiers. Lora and I had our own tent and I was given a uniform — a very affirming event for a small boy — and my job was to visit the men in the wards and chat to them. Many of them had some English and wanted to talk about India, and I had a growing sense that I was needed by them. Their eyes lit up when I came to their bedside and they told me about their families and their lives back home.

One of the soldiers asked me to scratch his leg as it was itchy, but when I looked I discovered there was no leg as it had been amputated as a result of his war injuries. He still felt the itch even though he had lost his leg. An incident like this makes a huge impact on a small boy. I was also challenged by the wonders of the Indian culture about which I was learning and the differences between this and my earlier Arabic, Jewish and English cultures.

> Living in Arabic, then the Jewish, English and Indian cultures makes one wonder who one really is

Identity requires affirming situations that impact our sense of belonging and sense of self, and all this can provide the personal affirmation needed.

In this book I examine what it means to be "me". I will look at the factors that contribute to a growing sense of self and see how we can maximise the positives in our lives and minimise the negatives. Our identity is formed by a number of factors: our experiences, by what people say to us and how they relate to us, by our successes and failures, and by the relationships that underpin our lives.

Questions for reflection or discussion

→ What influences can you identify in your life which have contributed to your sense of identity?

→ Can you recall particular incidents or people who impacted your life when you were very young?

→ Can you remember any incident in your own life which caused you to know that Jesus matters to you?

Chapter 2

Do I Really Matter?

*I matter most of all because God created me.
I matter to God and therefore to myself.*

My train was an hour late and when we reached the lay-by on the single-track railway, I saw the train coming up the line just ahead of us being blown up! It was a "goods train" carrying sheep and all but the engine was on fire as it rolled down the mountain slope. It was an awful sight watching sheep being burnt alive. But then I had an incredible thought: by running late we didn't hit the railway bomb which could have been planted for us! I was sorry about the sheep, but we were safe. Was this an answer to my prayer for safety as we boarded that train from Jerusalem to Cairo? I had already been saved from boarding a ship the previous year which was torpedoed, but more of this later. Though I often felt that no-one really cared about me, yet I was saved on more than one occasion from death and began to wonder if God wanted me to live.

When I eventually arrived in Australia I sensed that no-one was particularly interested in me. Most of the children in my class had never been overseas and, while I was open to talking about my Middle East and war experiences, they talked about their families, their pets and local sport. Their sense of self was rooted in their home life. I didn't have a home, nor did I have parents or siblings and I certainly knew nothing about Aussie sport! So I had nothing to talk about and felt an outsider. How I worked through some of these issues and how I discovered that while I did not seem to matter to anyone else, I did matter to God and ultimately to myself, I will share with you as we consider "who we really are".

A significant fact I discovered as I grew older was that I was made in God's image (*imago Dei*[1]). So let's examine how this impacts our self image.

Made in God's image

God created us as humankind.[2] This word "humankind" includes both male and female. "*God created humankind in his own image... male and female he created them*" (Genesis 1:27). The Genesis account goes on to demonstrate that the woman is part of man and the man is part of woman (Genesis 2:18–25). So neither men nor women are designed to function separately. Both are created as humankind, they are both in the divine image and neither is to be treated as an inferior person. The Hebrew Bible also highlights the very special work of God in this creative act by using two different words for creation of humankind. These words are translated in English as "created" and "made" (Genesis 1:26–27). The word "made" conveys the sense of fashioning what is created. God "fashioned" us giving us particular characteristics and abilities. We are not the same as the animals. We are not even a superior animal! We are a unique part of God's creation with unique capacities.

> There are **three** aspects to being in God's image: the **substantial** presence, the **functional** presence and the **relational** presence of God's image in us

All humankind is a special category of God's creation because God has imprinted on us his image, with the result that we are different from the rest of creation and we can reflect something of God's character to the rest of creation. This is an honour he has given us. This honourable status which God has endowed on all humanity gives rise to three exciting aspects in each one of us.

---

1 *Imago Dei* is the Latin phrase used for the "Image of God".
2 Most Bibles use the word "man", but this clearly refers to humankind as indicated in Genesis 1:27 "male and female he created them".

The first aspect is evident from the structural nature of humankind. This means that we are created with some of the Creator's attributes which make us "human": these include thought, reason, feelings, moral choice, dignity and freedom. These attributes set us apart from the rest of the animal world[3] because we have been fashioned to have these God-like capacities. This can be called the **substantial** presence of God's image in every human being.

The second aspect is that by creating us in his image he enables us to be his people in his world. We have been fashioned with the capacity to rule God's earth, to control much of creation and to use creation for our purposes (Genesis 1:28–31). So this is the **functional** presence of God's image in us and this means we have been given the ability to rule over much of creation as its stewards and to be creative in a variety of ways.

The third aspect is that God created us to be able to relate to him. This means that we are in communion with our Creator. We are his co-creators, his ambassadors as Paul tells the Corinthians:

> *Therefore we are ambassadors for Christ…working together with him. (2 Corinthians 5:20; 6:1)*

This can be called a **relational** presence of God's image in us. So we are not created just as a superior type of animal. Animals do not have a relationship with their Creator! We are able to creatively reflect the image of our Creator. However, being human we live in a world which encourages us not to be obedient to God and in fact we need God to call us into a continuing relationship with him. To establish this relationship we ask Jesus to forgive us for any rejection of him. This rejection is known as "sin". Having gained Jesus' forgiveness we seek to grow to be more and more Christ-like, so that our relationship starts to be reflected in how we function.

> **We are not created just as a superior type of animal**

---

3   This was argued by Aristotle in 347 BC in his *De anima*.

As I began to discover that I had these three capacities I began to see that *who I am* is centred in the incredible fact that God created and fashioned me and he sees me as someone of worth. God enjoys the fact that he created me and you, and he wants us to reflect to the world his image, which ideally means we reflect how wonderful he is (what Jude 24 calls God's presence in his glory and joy). We are people who can be in fellowship with God and we can have some impact in the world. He did not create us to be alone which is something I grasped as I grew older. I realised that we grow as individuals and gain a greater understanding about ourselves as we are in relationship with others and with God.

> We matter to God regardless of how we see God

Therefore, everyone is valuable to God. As we each determine who "we are", we are greatly enriched by knowing that we are important in God's eyes, that he loves each one of us and calls us to be in a relationship with him. We don't even have to believe in God. We matter to him regardless of how we see him. Of course he longs for us to respond to his love, but we are important in his eyes no matter what we think about him or what we feel about ourselves. What a privilege it is to know that we bear God's image!

Although I have no parents or siblings, was born in a foreign country and started life with another language, yet, regardless of my background, I know I belong to God and bear God's image. You also bear God's image, so how does this impact you?

Let's look more closely at what it means to be made in God's image and how this can help us in determining who we really are.

As we read Genesis chapters 1 and 2, we can see that as human beings we, along with all other humans, are the pinnacle of God's creation. We are the most wonderful part of his creative work. No act of creation follows the creation of humankind. We are God's final creative act, wonderfully created as an expression of God's own glory and joy. So the Genesis statement — *God created humankind in his own image* — means that regardless of what we think about God, we are created with some of the Creator's attributes. This is both the substantial and the functional presence of God's characteristics in us. But there is also the relational dimension available to us.

The relational aspect of being human

The New Testament builds on the Old Testament teaching about the relational presence of God's image in us by declaring that those who accept the Son of God, the Lord Jesus Christ as Saviour, are "in Christ" and he is "in us" (1John 2:5–6; John 17:20–24; 2 Corinthians 4:10–11). The connection between the biblical term of *being in the image of God and being Christ-like* is that we only start to understand the idea of God's image and Christ-likeness by getting to know Jesus. The New Testament declares that the Son of God is in the Father's image. So Paul tells the Colossian Church that Jesus *is the image of the invisible God* (Colossians 1:15); and the writer to the Hebrews states that God's Son

> *is the radiance of the glory of God and the exact imprint of his nature, and he upholds the universe by the word of his power. (Hebrews 1:3)*

Even if we do not accept Jesus as our Lord and Saviour, we still have the substantial and functional presence of God's image in us. But when we accept Jesus who is part of the triune Godhead and referred to as the Son of God, then we have the joy of a lively relationship with God. We then realise that in his strength we can be an adequate representation of God to the world over which God has told us to rule. As we seek to be Christ-like we are being faithful to our Creator in representing him. We are not physically like God since God has no known physical presence. Yet Jesus did have a physical presence when he walked this earth. While we do not look like him, we do want to care for people just as he did. So the term "image" refers not to appearance, but to the substantial nature of being human which is present in all humans and ideally the desire also to be in a relationship with God.

As we come to know Jesus and seek to grow to be like him we are starting to be Christ-like. As Paul said, we

> *are being transformed into the same image. For this comes from the Lord. (2 Corinthians 3:18)*

I discovered how important the study of the Scriptures was to help me discover what Christ-like characteristics I could develop. I found that God's written word[4] directs our goals, strengthens our faith in Jesus and develops our awareness of who we really are.

Our faith in Jesus may be a direct acceptance of this possibility, but for most the idea of "faith" and commitment to asking Jesus to be central to our lives come as we see God at work in our lives. I admit that this was easy for me, since I had already noted how I had been cared for as I was living with a family whose father was a doctor at a Christian hospital in Jerusalem. During this time I experienced two other incidents which affirmed for me a growing faith. The first incident was that the Government was planning to send me to England but the ship I was about to go on was torpedoed. The second incident was that the Matron of the hospital where I was living had been asked to take me and the young daughter of another British couple, who had also been killed, to England. The Matron said she could only take one child and took the girl. As that ship travelled across the Mediterranean Sea it also was torpedoed and the girl drowned, though the Matron survived. When we heard this news I thought, "Jesus wants me to stay alive" and so the picture of the "Shepherd and the lost lamb" became very real. Jesus was central to my life.

Since we are created to be in fellowship with our Creator, it becomes very evident that this relationship will contribute significantly to our self-esteem which is a major part of our identity. This relationship starts now as we live

---

4   It is also God the Holy Spirit who speaks to us usually through the Bible — Romans 8:14–15 — but also in our hearts and minds. The Bible teaches us that there is only one God who is one Being (or one in substance) and he eternally exists in three distinct Persons, namely Father, Son and Holy Spirit. This can be better understood when one notes that a triangle has three sides, but it is one triangle. Remove one side and there is no triangle! So God can be referred to as the triune God.

> Relationship with God can impact our self-esteem which is a major part of our identity

our earthly life and Christ's love continues to impact our thinking, our values, our emotions and our goals so that we keep growing to be more Christ-like, although we will only become entirely like Christ when we join him in his heaven.

Our faith is an expression of our eternal identity. Thus it makes clear that our self-image has developed in response to the wonderful fact that Christ is at work in each one of us and so we continue to "abide" in Jesus and he "abides" in us (John 15:5). This transformation to be increasingly Christ-like is a way of referring to the fact that we are created in God's image and have the capacity to reflect on what we do and the values we hold to. These capacities and values are our own personal assets. We have also been endowed with other assets namely: "thought, reason, feelings, moral choice, dignity, freedom, responsibility and relationship" and we will think about these assets in following chapters.

Questions for reflection or discussion

→ To what extent does the knowledge that we are made in God's image begin to answer the question 'Do I really matter?'

→ Outline some of the ways in which you can recognise in yourself the substantial, the functional and the relational image of God.

Chapter 3

In God's Image but Not Divine

We are not "the" image of God, but we are made "in" the image of God. We can grow to reflect the character of Christ.

While growing up in the Middle East I encountered some of the religious practices of local Muslim people. They knew that "God" (*Allah* in Arabic) was the Creator and assumed that they, as Muslims, represented Allah's expectations of all people. But when we discussed why, as Allah's representatives, they felt free to kill Zionists and the British they made it clear to me that people's lives were expendable if they were not following Allah as revealed by the prophet Mohammed. Now I know I was young, but I did attend Sunday School at Christ Church, Jerusalem which was just inside the Jaffa Gate, and I had learnt that I mattered because God had created me.

Years later I came to understand how very important it is to grasp the fact that not only did God make us, but also that he made everyone of us in his image and therefore everyone matters to God and so we matter to each other.

What I still had to learn was that I am not like God. Years later when working with some Muslims in Egypt I discovered that my Muslim friends saw themselves as "vice-regents" of Allah and thus responsible to judge people on behalf of Allah. This meant that they had a right to kill anyone who ignored Allah and his word as written in the Qur'an. It was then that I started to understand that I am not an earthly part of God. I am not divine. I am not God's vice-regent. Yet all humans are totally distinguished from the rest of creation. We are special. We have been created so as to be able to be in a relationship with God. God has invested us with his own characteristic of being "personal beings" with the capacity to relate to a personal God. It is this fact that we can relate to God and to others which defines our identity. We can know who we are because we relate to others but in particular because we can relate to our Creator. Our identity is rooted in relationships and particularly in being created in God's image. By being in his image we reflect to the world something of God's inter-personal characteristics.

Making a choice

The honour which God has given every human is to enable us to reflect to the world something of his existence. My Muslim friends wanted to show that Allah exists by promoting Allah's expectations about behaviour and punishing those who fail to respond. As a Christian I don't believe that God wants me to punish those who disobey him. We can choose to grow in Christ and increasingly reflect the attributes of Christ's character. As freedom is an essential part of God's identity as reflected by his free act of creation and since humans are created in God's image, all humanity has inherited some degree of freedom. Firstly, our freedom is limited, since we are not God, but we are free to choose to be a part of God's family. Secondly, we have inherited through the presence of Christ in our lives the liberty to choose not to sin, but to act in accordance with Christ's character. For this reason John writes in the New Testament:

> *So if the Son sets you free, you will be free indeed. (John 8:36)*

The picture in this passage is that we are not "slaves to sin", but we are free to choose to be children of God, to become members of the kingdom of God. These terms, "children of God" and "kingdom of God" are ways of outlining how we can belong to God. When Jesus walked this earth he said:

> *The kingdom of God has come near. Repent and believe the good news. (Mark 1:15 TNIV)*

This is the summons to everyone to respond to Jesus and accept his Lordship in our own lives. This declaration made by Jesus invites everyone to respond to him and this response is possible through his offer of forgiveness. The fact that freedom originates in Jesus and is offered by him shows that we can find true freedom in the person of Jesus.

However, we are also free not to choose to be part of the kingdom of God. Ignoring the source of our freedom, namely Jesus, means we are separated from God even though we still carry the honour which God has given us and enjoy the benefit of God's image in us.

Since freedom is part of our human identity we would want to exercise this. But our freedom is limited and this limitation helps us to realise that we are distinct from God. We are not some part of the divine. Regardless of our choice we do have in us God's image and so we

> **Real freedom comes through dependence on God**

have the freedom to relate across our own human boundaries and understand something about other people (all of whom matter to God), about creation and about God himself (Ephesians 1:13–14; Hebrews 4:12–13).

Our identity is rooted in the fact that we are created in God's image, but we cannot relate to God without being called and enabled by him. Clearly, it is God who wants us to be in a relationship with him and so he enables this to happen. As Paul tells the new Christians in Ephesus:

> *Adopted as sons [and daughters] through Jesus Christ according to the purpose of his will. (Ephesians 1:5)*

This freedom means that people are quite free not to believe in the existence of God or to presume that they do not need to be in a relationship with him. Yet they are still created in the image of God and are still responsible to share in the total human task of stewardship of the earth (Genesis 1:28). However, real freedom comes through dependence on God. This dependence does not mean we are destroying or limiting who we are, but rather that we are restoring our nature in the way we were created to be. Paul in his letter to the Galatian Christians writes:

> *For freedom Christ has set us free.*
> *We are sons and daughters redeemed by Jesus so that*
> *we are heirs of God's family. (Galatians 5:1 and a*
> *simplified version of 4:5–7)*

Failing to recognise where our powers come from and so failing to acknowledge the Creator of the whole earth is the fundamental nature of sin (Ephesians 2:1–10). Those who ignore God will be accountable for this rebelliousness against God, but even more than this, these people are failing to be the authentic human beings which God made them to be. We are authentically human by having a living relationship with our Creator. Since our nature is being created in the image of God, then our fulfilment as God's creation is found in belonging to our Creator; but to enjoy this status and to be authentically what God created us to be we need to accept his offer in Christ to be in a relationship with him.

The gift of God's grace

By recognising God as our God and as our personal Lord and Saviour we are responding to God's call for us to belong to him through the saving work of Jesus Christ. This means that God's grace is *given to each one of us according to the measure of Christ's gift* (Ephesians 4:7). We recognise this grace as we mature in our faith in Jesus. Grace is Christ's saving work in us and his "gift" is the on-going work of Christ in us such that we find ourselves reflecting his character. This is summed up by Paul in his letter to the Ephesian Church with the words that Jesus will

> *equip God's people for works of service, so that the body*
> *of Christ may be built up until we all reach unity in*
> *the faith and in the knowledge of the Son of God and*
> *become mature, attaining to the whole measure of the*
> *fullness of Christ. (Ephesians 4:12–13 TNIV)*

We are created as earthly persons, not divine persons. We are enabled to be God's fellow workers in his creation. This means we have a sanctity which no other creature has. For this reason we should treat each other as equals because every one of us (regardless of gender, race, appearance, abilities or faith) has the sanctity which God has given us as his creation. We can use this capacity for the benefit of creation or for its destruction.

Being in the image of God and responsible for creation, we are in partnership with God so long as we care for his creation and reflect the respect God has for all people. It is for this reason that we do not kill other people, although sadly we do get involved in wars. When a civilian is killed in the midst of a war this usually results in a court martial because governments recognise the command not to kill the unarmed. We treat, or should treat, all others with respect, whether they be our children, our spouse or our neighbour. Violence is not part of a Christ-like character and should not be part of the individual person's life. Each person is irreplaceable (Psalm 139:13; Isaiah 44:2). Each one of us exists, not by chance, but in relation with our Creator on whom we are dependent. So our attitude towards others should reflect a Christ-like way of relating to them.

We have already discussed relationships and noted that we can be in a living relationship with God and in a Christ-like relationship with others. It is God who created and honours us and therefore all people and we need to show this respect to them.

We give expression to relationships and to individual dignity through the exercise of *grace*. The spirit of grace comes from our Creator, it is part of God's character. Grace is the spontaneous gift of God and it consists of all his blessings in our eternal relationship with him: love, mercy, forgiveness, redemption, peace, strength and guidance. God demonstrates his grace by setting aside our failings and accounting us not on the basis of what we do or do not do, but on the basis of his compassionate merit. He will grant us forgiveness and calls us to follow and trust him. Grace can be defined as the unmerited goodness of God or the abundant blessing of God lavished on the undeserving. Paul summed this up in these words:

> *But God, being rich in mercy, because of the great love with which he loved us, even when we were dead in trespasses, made us alive together with Christ — by grace you have been saved ... this is not your own doing, it is the gift of God, not a result of works, so that no one may boast. (Ephesians 2:4–5, 8–9)*

It is goodwill that cannot be claimed as a right and cannot be earned! Grace is multi-faceted, full of richness and variety (1 Peter 4:10). It is Jesus who pours this into our lives — the *riches of God's grace that he has lavished on us* (Ephesians 1:7–8). It is an unearned gift granted to us as an expression of God's love for us. This gift of grace is expressed by Paul in writing to the Christian community in Rome:

> *All have sinned and fall short of the glory of God, and all are justified freely by his grace through the redemption that came by Christ Jesus. (Romans 3:23–24 TNIV)*

If our lives are centred on Christ and all he has done and is continuing to do for us, then our lives will radiate the faith, joy, gratitude, love and praise we have for the grace he has showered on us. We can ask ourselves whether we are showing forth God's grace in all we do and in our relationships in the home and in our day-to-day contacts (Colossians 3:12–14 and 4:5–6). We can also consider whether others can see the grace of God in our own lives and in the life of our church community.

Questions for reflection or discussion

→ What aspects of God's grace have you witnessed in your own life?

→ List some of the ways in which you can demonstrate God's grace to others.

→ In what practical ways can we radiate faith, joy, gratitude and love to others?

Chapter 4

What Are the Characteristics of Being Made in God's Image?

God has given us the capacity to reason, to feel and to make moral choices. He has also given us dignity, freedom, responsibility and relationships.

I was in Egypt for a few months waiting to board a troop ship carrying ANZACS who had fought in the North African sphere of the Second World War. I had been staying with a missionary family who had two children my age. The family discussed many issues: the local Islamic religion, the war and Christianity. I realised for the first time the importance of thinking through issues and how helpful it was to be able to discuss them with others. I also discovered the importance of relationships where we cared, not only for each other, but also for those around us, even those who did not agree with our Christian beliefs. Although I was just a child at the time, I found it stimulating to know that I had the capacity to reason and discuss issues with others.

So let's think about this capacity we have to reason and to feel for and about others.

Capacity to reason and feel

Our thinking powers may be obvious, yet it is a wonderful fact that we are able to think through issues and to have reasons for what we do, because

> Know and believe the love that God has for us. God is love, and whoever abides in love abides in God and God abides in him 1 John 4:16

reflecting, considering and decision-making are all part of God's gift to us. God is a thinking, decision-making God and he is the God of love. He has given these capacities to us. While humans have the ability to reason, God offers guidelines to help us think our way through to what he considers to be the truth. See Psalm 86:11 — *Teach me your way, O Lord, that I may walk in your truth.*

Another part of the substantial nature of being human is that we have emotions which are integrated with our capacity to reason, and this helps us to reflect on ourselves and to relate to others. This combination of reason and emotion enables us to determine that our identity will reflect some of God's nature, so that the Psalmist can write:

> *Righteousness and justice are the foundation of your throne; steadfast love and faithfulness go before you. (Psalm 89:14)* [5]

God wants us to determine for ourselves if we want him to be our God. He longs for us to respond to him, on the understanding that the basis for this relationship includes the principles of justice and righteousness and his commitment to love us unconditionally.

> For God so loved the world – John 3:16

His love for us is evident in a deep compassionate concern for us which ultimately is expressed by forgiving all who respond to him and thus he calls us to be part of his family. By investing love in us we are able to express love to others. Love for others means that others matter to us and we want to care for those in need. The principles of justice and righteousness determine how we relate to

---

5   See also Psalms 8, 19 and 34.

and regard other people just as God himself relates to us. We are not robots, we need to work out for ourselves if we will be obedient to God and determine for ourselves what type of identity we want to have. The call in these two Psalms, to learn from God and to be like him, means we want to make moral choices and thus can choose to be just and righteous.

Righteousness is God's gift to those who are obedient to him, whereas acting justly is our thoughtful, emotional and moral response. God wants us to be able to think about the world over which we are to rule (Genesis 1:36) and to do so justly (Jeremiah 23:5). He also wants us to exercise our capacity to feel great in ourselves and to have feelings for others by developing relationships with them and interacting with others so that there is a genuine partnership which is both thoughtful and emotional.

Moral decisions

How can we use our reasoning powers and our emotions to make moral decisions? Our moral decisions are probably rooted to some extent in the values which parents and other adults have given us. We have also been influenced by friends, often by books we have read, and perhaps by television programmes. Nevertheless, the actual capacity to make moral decisions is a capacity given to us by God. It is his hope that we will make the moral decision to be obedient to him and thus reflect in our character his righteousness as described in the Scriptures. For instance Amos records God's criticism of the spiritual blindness of his listeners and then goes on to indicate:

> *Let justice roll down like waters, and righteousness like an ever-flowing stream. (Amos 5:24)*

This is further explained by Micah in the challenge:

> *He has told you, O man, what is good; and what does the Lord require of you but to do justice and to love kindness, and to walk humbly with your God? (Micah 6:8)*

This ability to make righteous, moral decisions is part of God's creative act. In the texts above, "righteousness" is linked to "justice". This link is made because both words deal with making moral decisions about others and about ourselves. These words underline the fact that we have an obligation to act justly towards others and to treat them with the dignity they deserve as people whom God loves and who are created in his image. In the New Testament Jesus further explains righteousness by teaching the crowd how they should function. Clearly Jesus expected his listeners to make moral choices as outlined in the Beatitudes (Matthew 5).

One example of the impact that following Jesus can make is seen in the action of Zacchaeus who, after meeting personally with Jesus, made a moral decision about repaying defrauded people (Luke 19:1–9).

Maybe we could pause and reflect on what changes we could make in our own lives and attitudes if we allowed the "justice" of God to affect what we do.

Now, what about this word "dignity"?

Dignity

We've considered that the ability to think, to feel and to make moral choices means we are decision-makers. This adds to the sense of the worth of every person and gives us a God-given capacity unlike the rest of God's creation. The word *dignity* draws attention to the awareness that everyone is valuable before God. The attitude of regarding others with dignity regardless of how they look or whatever they happen to be doing, is a learned capacity. It may not be easy to think of people we do not like or people who follow a different religion as being the object of God's love, but they and we are responsible to show forth God's love. We might do this by meeting a need or by showing kindness in some practical way.

> Everyone has dignity and everyone should treat others with dignity

A few years ago my wife, Robyn, was ministering to people in a refugee camp in Eastern Europe. The people were very poor and all had lost their homes in recent inter-ethnic fighting. Since the organisers had no money to provide lunch after the meeting, each person was asked to bring their own lunch. Robyn, as a visitor, had no lunch with her and when she had finished speaking, an elderly, frail woman came up to her, opened her handbag, and gave Robyn her own lunch. It was an orange! That was all the woman had, but she gave it away to say "thank you" to a visitor. Although Robyn and the woman could not speak the same language, the kind gesture provided a special link which resulted in a hug of thanks. This woman, who had no possessions or material goods, revealed a God-given dignity as she selflessly met the need of someone else.

> God affirms our dignity and our worth by loving us

We gain our dignity from God regardless of what we think about him. He has affirmed each one of us as the object of his love (John 3:16). Everyone, regardless of abilities, ethnicity or different world views, is therefore equal before God and must be seen as equal before us. It is God who affirms our dignity and our worth by loving us. He is the heavenly Father who promises eternal life for all who believe in him (Romans 3:21-24). Calling God "Father" (for instance, in the Lord's prayer) is a way of declaring the relationship we are called to have with God. Thus we can refer to ourselves as God's children (John 1:12) and this strengthens the awareness of our relationship with God through Jesus. We may lack affirmation from parents or others, but we know that God affirms us and we matter to him. In my own case, although I was orphaned as a baby and never had parental care, as a teenager in times of loneliness I sang to myself the chorus, "Jesus loves me this I know" and affirmed that even when I had no one else to love me, Jesus cared about me and I mattered to him. This was the affirmation of my dignity which I needed.

To believe or to have faith in Jesus means that we simply accept his free gift of salvation, repent of what we have done wrong and allow him to be our Lord and Saviour. We serve his purposes in the world both by caring with dignity for creation and by representing his character with dignity to the world. In doing this we are standard bearers of the just and righteous God referred to above. Without us the people of the "world" may not know that there is a God — they probably will not know that he cares and calls them to belong to him. If we are not involved in his creation then this must mean that we do not care about the wonder and dignity of his handiwork (Psalm 19). In demonstrating God's dignity we will also want to exercise our own responsibility to act on issues of human rights and justice.

Dignity in humanity is not determined by the attitude of others or by the State. It is a feature of the intrinsic worth of all humanity. All humans are created by God and even if they ignore him this does not remove from them the dignity which God has given them as his creation. Our dignity includes the creative power which can show itself as we create and develop ideas. God has affirmed himself as the great Creator and he has affirmed us. We all matter to him.

Each one of us individually shares in God's dignity, but Christians as a community are also to reflect this. This is explored by Paul in his letters to the Corinthians and the Ephesians, as he explains that the Holy Spirit is at work among the Christians for "the common good" (1 Corinthians 12:7) and there is a unity the Christians have in Christ (Ephesians 4:3). We, both individually and collectively, have a challenging position in the world in representing the righteousness and justice of God, to be managers of creation and to represent the dignity which God has given to humanity. This brings together the functional and the relational aspects of God's image in us as outlined earlier.

Another of the consequences of this dignity is that all people are in the image of God and have certain rights. Although some countries fail to identify these rights, the rights still exist regardless of the laws of the land. Whatever laws do exist, they should reflect the dignity of each person. Rights may be removed by some authorities because of the world view and political ideology held, but individuals usually agonise over the loss of any of these rights. With the rights there are also responsibilities. These responsibilities may be specified in the laws of the nation and the customs of the people. For those who are pursuing a relationship with God, responsibilities are outlined in the ten commandments, such as responding to God as our creator and Lord, honouring parents, refraining from lying, stealing, and from coveting what others have.

Government laws and practice should provide protection so that the rights and dignity of each person are respected. People can sometimes exercise power over others and take the opportunity to be intimidating, over-demanding or destructive of another person who is deemed to be weaker or subordinate. The act of bullying others means that the dignity of the other is being ignored. It also means that the bully lacks personal dignity, because this person has reduced his/her character to be one which lacks the capacity to care about others and which needs to be strengthened by having power over others. Once we recognise this lack of care we realise that our capacity to care and to think of others as significant people is a capacity which emerges from the fact that God created us and each one of us is significant. Because God created us, we should respect and esteem everyone. This is their right to be treated with dignity and it is our right to grant them respect.

> **Power over others is dangerous**

Another factor which can help us to develop our capacity to show dignity to others is that God treats us with dignity. He wants each one of us to be his children. He wants each one of us to be a member of his family forever. The term "family" is used only once in the New Testament and it conveys the sense that God is our father and so we are his children and members of his family (Ephesians 3:14–15); we are also referred to as God's children in other passages like Romans 8:14–17. God's dignity can be understood as we acknowledge his majesty, his all-knowing almightiness and that he freely created the world. Furthermore, he is everywhere, he is eternal and infinite, yet remains personally addressable.

Let's read the next chapter to think about the impact of freedom, responsibility and relationships in the formation of our identity.

Questions for reflection or discussion

→ Reflect on any moral choices you are facing at the moment.

→ What influences can you identify that have already provided you with a "moral compass" for making decisions?

→ Can you identify one person towards whom you acted without recognising that person's dignity, and how could you in future possibly respond in a more Christ-like way?

Chapter 5

The Beauty of Relationships

Now let's look at freedom, responsibility and relationships.

I made some friends when I first arrived in Australia and went to a boarding school for my primary education, but in high school I found making friends much more difficult. This was partly because I didn't want to share with others that I was lonely. While I saw others going home to families at the end of the school day, I was "baby-sitting" a house on my own in a cold country town. I was certainly free and not responsible to anyone, but I had no family and no friends. The only thing that kept me going was knowing that I mattered to God and was in a relationship with him through Jesus.

Freedom

I knew even then that the reason why we can have a productive relationship with God is because he has created us to function as free people and be responsible for our thinking and our actions. Even though I was on my own I knew I had the capacity to make decisions about my life. My understanding of freedom and responsibility has increased since then so let me share some of this with you.

When God is spoken of as the First and the Last (*Alpha and Omega* in Revelation 1:8; 22:13) we have evidence of the eternal nature of God. The fact that God is also in control of the very beginning and the very end of all life shows that he is not under the pressure of any other force: he has absolute control and hence he is free. This infinite freedom is made clear by Paul in Colossians 1:16–17 referring to Jesus Christ,

> *For by him all things were created, in heaven and on*

> *earth, visible and invisible… and he is before all things, and in him all things hold together.*

In this freedom God created the world and placed humanity in the world, creating people in his image. This image is foundational to being human since it reflects on the *relational aspect* already mentioned. God is a free agent able to do whatever he wants to do and free to be in a relationship with us, all of which is consistent with his character and his wishes for his creation. He is free from sin and his moral excellence is revealed, not only in his character, but also in all his works (Exodus 15:12; James 1:13; Revelation 4:8; 15:4). His infinite power and his will, as well as his independence and his decision to create and sustain the world and us, are all evidence of his freedom. He has given us freedom to choose to belong or not to belong to him. We also have some freedom in using our abilities, but we may be constrained by our political, social and economic environments, as well as by our friendships. So we are not as free as we would like to be! Yet part of the image of God in us is the freedom he has given us. It is a freedom we have in Christ:

> *For freedom Christ has set us free; stand firm therefore and do not submit again to a yoke of slavery. (Galatians 5:1)*

This is really freedom from behaving in a way that is not acceptable to God nor helpful to others.

> *…the fruit of the Spirit is love, joy, peace, patience, kindness, goodness, faithfulness, gentleness, self-control; against such there is no law. And those who belong to Christ Jesus have crucified the flesh with its passions and desires. (Galatians 5:22–24)*

The fact that the Holy Spirit can give us gifts which reflect the character of Christ, and the fact that we have the ability to think, is evidence of the freedom we do have, even though our freedom may be severely limited in some situations.

As I grew up I discovered that my freedom is a very significant aspect of my identity. It allows me to be strong about my self-image. It allows me to reflect on my relationship with God and with others. I can also consider my political and philosophical world view because of the freedom God has given me. This is part of the substantial presence of God's image in me as discussed earlier.

I have visited many parts of the world where people do not have freedom and are controlled in almost every area of their lives by authorities who dictate what they can believe and do and who they can relate to. Let's consider how the absence of freedom might affect us if we found ourselves in a situation like this.

If I lived in a society where I did *not* have freedom and was regulated by the community institutions and world view, or made to be subservient to those in power, then both my identity and my freedom to relate to whomever I want to relate to would be limited by these external forces. I might be forced to function in ways which did not reflect my true identity. I might develop a resistant element in my identity and so may look for ways to express this resistance in opposition, antagonism or even aggression.

While these conditions can exist in a dictatorial political society, the lack of freedom can also occur in some institutions to which I might belong. Where there is an absence of such freedom through an authoritarian environment I might reformat my identity so as to cope with these demands. While I have some personal authority in myself and in my choices, nevertheless, the removal of these choices limits and reshapes my identity and the way I might function.

Responsibility

We are *responsible* people. This is evident in the instructions to Adam who was told from which tree he could not eat (Genesis 2:16–17). Yet the tree was there, so he could decide to act responsibly or to act irresponsibly by being

> When you grow up with no family you can lack an understanding of permanent relationships. I think I gained some idea of a relationship on that one occasion when I saw the picture of Jesus and the lost lamb

disobedient to God's instructions. We are not forced to act in certain ways. God did not make Adam and Eve act in certain predetermined ways. He gave Adam and Eve freedom to choose to act responsibly or irresponsibly and they chose the latter! They chose to eat "*the fruit of the tree of the knowledge of good and evil*" (Genesis 2:17) albeit under verbal pressure from the serpent. The fact that God came and met with them and accused them of disobeying his instruction shows us that they were responsible for their action. So we can see from this story that we also are created to be responsible people. For me it is a wonderful fact that we are created in God's image, which means we are not robots, but we enjoy the benefit of God's freedom with the result that we have the freedom to choose between good and evil in most situations. We, like Adam and Eve, are free to act responsibly or irresponsibly towards ourselves, towards other people and towards God. This means we are free to be in an obedient relationship with God or to ignore him.

Relationships

We have seen that God has called us to be in a *relationship* with him. As we read about Abraham and the children of Israel we note that God calls on these people as a nation to know him and be obedient to him. Their relationship with God was defined by a special agreement otherwise known, in the Old Testament, as the "covenant". Now we may know the word "covenant" in legal terms, and this word is used by God also in a legal sense. Covenant as defined by God is explained in his promises to his people and their response is to be in an obedient relationship with him. The covenant is outlined by God in the ten commandments (Exodus 20). In the New Testament the covenant is defined for us in terms of obedience (Romans 6:1–14; Hebrews 8:8–11). We are being true to ourselves if we live by God's law. This law can still be referred to in the words of the ten commandments, but the NT focuses our attention on our relationship with Jesus and requests us to live in a Christ-like fashion (Matthew 5, 6 and 7).

We know God's law through the Scriptures (Ephesians 1:13–14). We can act responsibly and we are free to be obedient to this covenant so that our authentic identity reflects the character of Jesus Christ. We need to grow in our knowledge of Jesus through the study of the Bible. God did not create us only to rule over the earth — the substantial dimension of our humanness. He created us also to belong to him and to one another (the relational dimension). If we fail to see ourselves in these personal relationships we are in fact not being really human, because our humanness is forged by being in living relationships.

We can live with God eternally or we can reject this relationship and be separated from God eternally. It is interesting that creatures live by instinct, but humans to some extent live by choice. We can choose to obey God's will or we can choose to go our own way. We give expression to this relationship by acknowledging him as God, and more particularly as our God. Failure to accept God as God does not remove from such people the power God has given them to *"fill the earth and subdue it"* (Genesis 1:28). However, we can go beyond this basic functional aspect on the basis of a *relationship with God*. So Paul can say to the Colossian church with full confidence:

> Animals live by instinct – humans live by choice

> *Put on then, as God's chosen ones, holy and beloved, compassionate hearts, kindness, humility, meekness and patience, bearing with one another... forgiving each other, as the Lord has forgiven you... And let the peace*

> *of Christ rule in your hearts... Let the word of Christ dwell in you richly... And whatever you do, in word or deed, do everything in the name of the Lord Jesus, giving thanks to God the Father through him. (Colossians 3:12–17)*

We can see from this letter to the Colossians that Paul links God and the Lord Jesus. As Jesus himself stated *"I and the Father are one"* (John 10:30). So here already is a relationship. Jesus went on to say *"the Father is in me and I am in the Father"* (v.38). The relationship is further amplified in the letter to the Hebrews:

> *God spoke to our fathers by the prophets, but in these last days he has spoken to us by his Son... through whom also he created the world. He is the radiance of the glory of God and the exact imprint of his nature... (Hebrews 1:1–3)*

So the better we know Jesus the better we know God. Paul goes on to caution us that we should,

> *Walk in wisdom... Let your speech always be gracious, seasoned with salt, so that you may know how you ought to answer each person. (Colossians 4:5–6)*

In these ways we are being responsible (*"walk in wisdom"*) reflecting the very character of Christ (*"gracious, seasoned with salt"*). So in our relationship with others, we are to reflect Christ's righteousness. This means that we function as a person who has been made righteous through the presence of Jesus in our lives (Leviticus 11:44; 1 Peter 1:13–16; Hebrews 10:10). We also grow in righteous behaviour as we absorb the teaching of the Bible and so see in ourselves the power of God's written word discerning our thoughts and intentions (Hebrews 4:12).

Paul makes it clear that when we function as a righteous person we are *"created after the likeness of God in true righteousness and holiness"* (Ephesians 4:24).

In other words, the fact that we have been created in the image of God is now strengthened by acting and speaking in ways which reflect Christ's righteousness. This does not mean that we no longer do something wrong, something which is against God's character, but it does mean that because of our relationship with God and our commitment to repent, he forgives us and accounts us as righteous people. So our identity is to reflect a Christ-like character as we seek to be obedient to his will.

It is a real challenge to us all that when Mahatma Gandhi was asked by the missionary E. Stanley Jones about his stance against Christianity he replied, "Oh, I don't reject Christ. I love Christ. It's just that so many of you Christians are so unlike Christ".[6]

Since our *growing* character should be reflecting the character of Christ, we need to grow in our love for God who loves us, and then we can increasingly *"love one another"* (1John 4:7). Our creation in the image of God gives us this unique ability, enabling us to care for others. God cares for us and he has prepared us for a long-term future with him, but he wants us to choose this. As we look towards this long-term future we can think about growing in Christ-likeness, which occurs fully when we enter heaven.

Now that we know that being made in the image of God means being in a relationship with him, and we have reflected on the consequences of this relationship, let us consider next how this affects our identity and our growing sense of self.

---

6   From a speech by Ghandi to Women Missionaries in 28 July 1925. www.youtube.com/watch?v=ItJN_u7WD00

Questions for reflection or discussion

→ Reflect on the variety of relationships you currently have. What effect do these have on you?

→ What do you think is needed to keep those relationships strong?

Chapter 6

Self-Esteem and How Others See Me

We have noted how God sees us as his creation and that we are able to be in relationship with him. This means that our value and our sense of self-worth are because God gives us this worth.

When I got to university I was faced with a number of questions. How much would I have to tell the scholarship officer about myself? Could I ask for full financial support on the grounds that I was a war orphan? How confident would I be in telling my story? Fortunately my anxiety was fairly quickly allayed when I found him interested and sympathetic, agreeing to give me the financial support I needed. A desire to make some friends also resulted in my facing some other questions. Would I mix with the drinking crowd or with the debating team or one of the other clubs or would I join one of the Christian groups? I decided that as a significant part of my identity was being a Christian I would join the Christian Union. This was an important decision as it provided me with wonderful Christian fellowship and with friends, some of whom I have had for life. As a result of my involvement in the Evangelical Union I became a committee member with responsibility for overseas students. By now I was living at a hostel for international students and was making friends with students from many different parts of the world. I was developing friendships that would significantly impact my identity.

Our self-esteem is our evaluation of ourselves

When we think about ourselves we note our skills, our beliefs, our values, our ability to manage ourselves and our emotions, as well as our ability to develop friendships. But how do we think others regard us? We are constantly assessing ourselves in relation to other people. I know that I feel great when someone thanks me for the talk I have just given. It helps me to know that some others have accepted my comments and thus have accepted me. When there are no "thank-you" comments I feel I haven't done well and my self-esteem drops. The way others see us and relate to us will impact the way we think about ourselves. A low self-esteem means we wish we were different, and this may be an outworking of how we see others and think others see us. A healthy self-esteem indicates that we accept ourselves as we really are — God's very special creation — even if others are not affirming us as much as we would like!

Lack of affirmation may be a reason why we may not feel good about ourselves and as a result our self-esteem can be adversely affected. If we are bullied at school, or at home, or "put down" by a more senior person at work, our self-image can be seriously diminished. But it doesn't really matter what others think of us. What does matter is that God loves us and has created us to be a person he values and to whom he has given unique qualities. Each one of us is the object of Christ's concern: whether we are children (Mark 10:13–16), a person with authority (Matthew 8:5–13), a labourer (Matthew 4:18–22), a lost person (like the prodigal son, Luke 15: 3–7 and 11–24), or a bureaucrat (Luke 5:27–31 and 11:37)!

Have you noticed that our view of ourselves can change from time to time depending on whether we are confident in a given situation? Those with a positive self-esteem have a favourable opinion of themselves and seem to be

> If you need a greater sense of self-confidence read the three goals here about ways you can strengthen your self-confidence

confident in almost any situation. But that may not always be the case! They may actually have low self-confidence in areas of activity which are outside their "comfort zone". So don't let's compare ourselves with people who seem confident all the time — they may, like us, feel quite inadequate in some situations.

So, where do we go from here? Our starting point — ***our first goal*** — could be to recognise that self-esteem is the result of self-respect gained from our standing before our Creator. We believe in ourselves because God created us. This is the substantial aspect of being created in God's image referred to earlier. We matter to God. This is a wonderful source of encouragement even though we might not get the recognition we would like to have from those we hoped would affirm us! What really matters is that we know that our self-esteem is an outcome of being created in God's image.

The ***second goal*** is to note our strengths and our weaknesses. In this way we are being obedient to the Scriptures for as Peter says:

> *Each one of you should use whatever gift you have received to serve others, as faithful stewards of God's grace in its various forms. (1 Peter 4:10 TNIV)*

At the same time we are to think of ourselves in a balanced way:

> *Do not think of yourself more highly than you ought, but rather think of yourself with sober [realistic] judgement, in accordance with the faith God has distributed to each of you. (Romans 12:3 TNIV)*

We are not proud since the base for our self-affirmation is God, not ourselves. Whatever gifts we have inherited or developed are God's gifts to us.

It took me a while to determine what my gifts were and it was often in accepting a new responsibility or in responding to new opportunities that I discovered that there were some things that I could do reasonably well. Then, of course, I had to develop those gifts by using them!

If we recognise that God is the basis for our self-affirmation, then the ***third goal*** is our response — a response in faith to Jesus Christ. Faith is a word which sums up our attitude of trusting Jesus, through whose death on the cross and resurrection we gain the status of being accounted forgiven and a member of his family (Acts 16:30–31; John 5:24).

In this faith we present our weaknesses and our strengths to God and recognise that we are growing people — hence the need for "sober judgement". We can grow through our weaknesses by identifying them, and in prayer ask God to help us to grow through them and so develop our strengths. What is important is that we recognise the weaknesses while at the same time noting our strengths, and so face with renewed vigour the challenges and difficulties of life. In this way we clarify our identity and avoid becoming lost in the problems of life or in the criticisms of others. At the same time we have affirmed the relationship aspect of being in God's image.

The search for self-esteem can be both fragile and powerful

Thinking about ourselves may not be easy because:

* We tend to listen to others some of whom may be critical of us and we view ourselves in the light of their evaluation.
* We want to make an assessment of ourselves by recognising our gifts and also acknowledging our weaknesses and this can be difficult.
* We know what we are capable of doing and when there are no opportunities for us to use our gifts we might begin to doubt if we really do have these gifts.

As we identify our gifts we develop an awareness of our identity. It is this identity which will enable each one of us to also view ourselves as having power alongside of others and sometimes power over the implementation of ideas.

It is important to recognise that as a person I am equal to everyone else regardless of roles, gender or ethnicity. Therefore, I will not allow others to minimise me. I am free to listen to their comments, which may emerge out of the various roles which others have, such as a medical practitioner or a person with a given authority. Yet, since I know who I am and what my values are, I am both free and powerful enough to respond to others and to ideas as I wish. I may feel fragile because of negative comments or because of legal or social requirements which I need to accept or to reject in accordance with any institutional specifications, but I am powerfully "me" and capable of responding as I desire. It is my attitude to the institutions and the roles others have which will give meaning and strength to my own life and thus make my identity clear — at least to myself!

Let's try some thoughts: Who am I?

- I am God's person in his world.
- I am in fellowship with God through my faith in Jesus Christ and can talk to Jesus through prayer.
- I am unique, no one else is like me.
- I am confident in certain situations and ill at ease in others.
- I know my weaknesses and will seek to mature in these areas.
- I react in appropriate or inappropriate ways to certain activities, ideas or people and may need to work on this.
- I can be very calm in some areas of life.
- I hold to certain values and philosophies and out of these I have developed and continue to develop my capacity to think about issues. Some of my thinking will also be moulded by people I meet.
- I have been given certain gifts which I will seek to use.
- I am ME! – not my friend, nor my neighbour.

As I identify that "I am ME" — unique, special, an individual loved and honoured by God — I recognise that I am different from others — from other members of my family and different from other people I meet. What other people who matter to us say about us will impact our self-image, but it is all the factors listed above which will determine our self-esteem. Many of the memories of our past, as a child, as a pupil, as a teenager and then as an adult will be recalled and will have some influence on determining our self-image. This understanding of ourselves will help us determine our decision to undertake or not undertake certain tasks, and will help us determine with which groups we may or may not associate at depth. There are other numerous activities over which we can make a determination and these activities will impact our self-image. Our behavioural practices, our hobbies and interests, any fears or joys we may have, and our circle of friends will all shape us in some way and will help to mould who we are and determine how we see ourselves. However, let's be alert in case any of these contributing factors to our "being" are making us into someone we don't want to be.

> Our friends can impact our development. They can influence the image we have of ourselves

Am I always "me" or do I change over time?

The changes we see in other people over a number of years are often a result of the changes in the groups to which each belongs. Group culture can be very influential. Others in any group to which we belong can have a helpful influence on our personal development. Yet others can generate in us unhelpful values and hence make us into the sort of person we would prefer not to be. The relationships we have, the images we absorb from the media, the level of trust we have in our family and friends, the way we see our own body, our values as well as the success or otherwise of the tasks we perform all have an influence on us. While some of these factors change over time and may produce changes in us, nevertheless each one of us is the same essential person throughout life. We have the same identity yet we are developing people. Let's go a little further in the next chapter to see how this can be.

Questions for reflection or discussion

→ What are the positives — people or events — that have contributed to your sense of self-worth to this point?

→ If your sense of self is fairly fragile or not clearly formed at this stage, reflect on what you might do about this.

Chapter 7

Identity Has Continuity

Our self-esteem, our relationships, the way we see ourselves as well as our values all contribute in establishing who I am. My self-image is formed by how I see myself and how I think others see me.

The real me

Have you ever wondered whether you are the same person you were when you were a child or a teenager? Am I the same person as the boy who lived in Jerusalem all those years ago? Yes, we are the same person! Circumstances may change, situations may change, influences on us may change, but basically I am the unique person I was when I was born and that doesn't change. I am always the same person notwithstanding the different countries I have lived in and regardless of the different influences on my life. Even the way I have behaved or the way I have thought in different circumstances over the years does not change the fact that I am the same person.

How others see me, my relationships and my values, may change from time to time, yet my identity, that is *who I am*, is the same. What lies behind all these factors is *"the real me"*. This is my identity. I have continuity. I am the same person. I have a past, a present and a future. No matter what changes occur in my life, in my behaviour or in my thinking I am always "myself". Changes come because of new experiences, different circles of friends, changes in ideas and values, as well as increasing age. Some people may say after a conversion experience, "I have a new status before God and I am a new person". Certainly these people have a new status before God because they have become a child of God and a member of the kingdom of heaven. With this declaration such a person looks forward to that ultimate time when he or she joins Jesus in heaven. But what does such a person mean by saying, "I am a new person"?

What they are really saying is "my new relationship with Jesus, my Saviour and God, strengthens my identity — I now know in a fresh way who I am because I have become part of God's family". But what they now will need to do is allow God to change some aspects of their lives, values, attitudes and relationships to reflect that new status. This requires a decision of the will and may result in some significant changes in life style.

I recall seeing this happen with a high school student in the Solomon Islands. I went there to start Scripture Union/Inter-School Christian Fellowship (ISCF) and invited school students to a camp. One boy was an excellent sports person, but he got drunk on the weekends and other boys tried to copy him. He came to the camp and discovered that real joy is in belonging to Jesus. His conversion was dramatic! The others at the camp were very surprised. He went back to school and started an ISCF group and told the students that getting drunk was the beginning of a down-hill road. He attracted half the school to the ISCF meetings and began to concentrate more in class with the result that he achieved better results. The School Principal told me what an enormous change had occurred and what a wonderful new role model he now was for others. He finally gained a scholarship to the university in Fiji where he started the Christian Fellowship. He had changed some aspects of his behaviour, but his unique identity as a person was still the same. What a difference a relationship with Jesus can make!

> What a change can occur such as in this boy in the Solomon Islands

Now let's explore some words which can help us understand ourselves and our identity a little further. These are *transparency, past experiences, belonging* and *respect*.

Transparency

How we see ourselves will have an enormous impact on how we function as people. The main features of our identity are the same, but some aspects of how we express ourselves and who our friends are may change. At various stages of our early lives we may be told who we are and how to behave. Then as we become teenagers, we seek to determine our own identity. As adults we seek to develop an understanding of "self" and we may need to set aside how we think others have viewed us in the past.

> Transparency is necessary but makes us vulnerable

It is helpful to know that to gain support requires a willingness to share with others something of ourselves, even if the amount of information we decide to share is limited. Transparency reveals something of the uniqueness of each person. It can also make us vulnerable as we are opening up ourselves to the scrutiny of others. It is this identity which reveals the contribution each can make to our circle of friends and to our community or work place. We want others to "see" who we really are. It does take time to discover, accept and affirm who we are regardless of what others think about us. Deciding which values and world view we will adopt as our own strengthens our own identity.

Past experiences

What has happened to us in the past will impact our identity. It is possible that the way parents or other adults treated us in childhood will have an influence on us as adults. We cannot fully escape our history. I cannot escape being an orphan or growing up in a time of war. If other adults regard us as inadequate in our studies or in our contribution to home or society, we may well decide that we have to prove ourselves by doing better in some activity. As adults we may decide to add qualifications to our name as evidence of our gifts. We may determine that some negative aspects of our childhood or teenage years can be set aside in adulthood or we may seek help to work them through.

> Our childhood experiences need not determine our adult behaviour

We may seek to overcome the lack of love or of affirmation by absorbing the fact that Jesus loves us and cares about us and as a consequence we may begin to care about ourselves. In fact, our capacity to love others is likely to be parallel to our capacity to care for ourselves (Matthew 22:39).

As adults we continue to grow as persons. We seek to respond to our past experiences by facing our hopes, fears, joys and doubts. Yet in the midst of this we will hold fast to our identity, modifying those aspects of our behaviour which we know need to be developed.

Belonging

Identities are partly formulated by ethnicity. This includes race, language and nationality. Most of us like to belong to our school, or church, or some other group as well as feel that we belong to our country. One aspect of belonging to the nation is by reflecting in what we say or do something that is in the popular arena, such as a sporting event or a national world view, if there is one. Changes in national political status can be a cause of disruption in our own status. For instance, in Eastern Europe the communist political theories dominated the thinking and behaviour of people in those countries until the 1990s. Then the breakdown in the "Communist" world view caused many to be "lost". They had lost something of their identity which was rooted in the Communist philosophy. Suddenly this philosophy of life and relationships was threatened as being no longer relevant. A new basis for their values was required and for those who had no Christian base it was very difficult to find a new foundation for their identity and for a personal value system. This can be seen to some extent among the Aboriginal people of Australia, where their value system rooted in their "dreamtime" concepts and "land-markers" was taken away by the "white/western" milieu around them. They no longer had a basis for their identification as a unique people living in their own world with their own world view. They were forced to develop a new identity, not only reducing the significance of their tribal inheritance, but seeing themselves as Australians. The new western world view has proven to be difficult for many to adopt.

Identity is a challenge for those whose physical features reveal an ethnicity which is not that of the local majority. The continuity of our ethnicity cannot be escaped even though there may be a strong desire to be different. For instance, an Asian adopted by an Australian couple and living in Australia or an Asian living with his or her own parents, but growing up in Australia, so often wants to be seen as an Australian. On the other hand, some adult migrants like to maintain their ethnic background and want others to recognise this. One way of asserting this is by dressing in accordance with the person's religious standing and so more strongly declaring both the ethnic and the religious background. Religious clothing or symbols become an alternative value system as a base for publicly stating both one's ethnic and religious culture and thus one's inherited identity. However, it can reduce a sense of belonging to the community. Through friendship we can often help others to see more of themselves and more about us than just one or two obvious features. While the response of others may be a problem, we need to realise that it is up to us to help them see more of who we are. Our identity is more than just our appearance: it has developed though our life experiences, it reflects our values and provides a base for relating to others.

> What is important to you? What view of life do you hold to? Which values really matter to you? Who is the most important person in your life?

Respect

We need to treat others with the respect they deserve since we need to view them as God views them, as people worthy of his love and his work of creation. No matter what view we hold about creation, the important fact for the Christian is that the whole of creation proclaims the glory of God. The creation of you and of me is a manifestation of God's love and so we need to treat each other with respect.

By showing respect for others, we are acknowledging that they are created in God's image. This is the most important fact about "who I am" and who they are. They are human, they are unique and each has a unique identity. This identity is a declaration that I and they are different from everyone else. Yet at the same time I discover myself in relation to other people and in the context of the local culture. I may want to be better looking, or more able in a particular area, but I know what and who I am. Others may view me differently from the way I see myself because they may focus on other factors such as my ethnicity, my appearance, my accent, or the things I do. The word "identity" has a large range of meanings and is influenced by:

* ethnicity, gender, race, language, personal abilities
* achieved activities, friendships, family life
* political commitments, recognition, authority
* role responsibilities at work and in the community.

At each point in my life others may see me differently from the view I have of myself, but that will be their assessment of my identity. Regardless of their assessment I continue to be "ME".

Questions for reflection or discussion

→ If I am always "ME" even though I change and mature over time, it could be helpful to make a list of your gifts/interests/characteristics and the relationships which make you, "You".

→ Better still, ask someone else to write down the good things they see in you. This can be very affirming.

Chapter 8

The Social Self

*Relationships are central for our self-image,
for our sanity and for our emotions.*

The community with which we are connected

The first time I went to the Pacific Island of Samoa to start the work of Scripture Union I was met by the local pastor whom I had met briefly on another island. I stayed with his family, sleeping on the timber floor with its thatched roof. The whole family lived in this "fale". No-one seemed to own anything beyond a few clothes and a Bible. When I opened the Bible I saw lots of names written in the front page. I asked about this and was told that everyone in the village belonged together and so the Bible was shared and those who kept it for a period of time would often write their name in it, and so strengthen the sense that they all belonged together. I came to discover the enormous ways in which the people of the village saw themselves belonging together and sharing with one another their interests, their joys and some sadness. Samoans have a strong sense of their nationhood, even though they are a very small nation (190,000 people).

This is a great example of the fact that we are not people in a vacuum. We develop our identity as we reflect on ourselves through the relationships we have. The meaning we give to these relationships and the experiences we have in these social settings are determined by our value system, our faith position and the decisions we have made about ourselves, such as what sort of people we want to be.

We are created so as to be able to communicate with our Creator. God himself is in a relationship of Father, Son and Holy Spirit. This becomes evident in the New Testament (John 14). This relationship shows us that love is expressed, that there is communication between each one in the Godhead, and that there is communication with us. This communication includes forgiveness, acceptance and long-term commitment. So we are created to be able to communicate with other people, to be able to give and accept or reject the love of others, to be able to choose with whom we will seek to have a short or a long-term relationship.

The parable of the prodigal son and his father demonstrates the need for a relationship, the capacity to forgive and the desire for commitment (Luke 14). It is very difficult to live entirely on one's own, and those who are placed in such lonely situations, such as in prison for a long period of time, are often adversely affected by it. We are social beings and need to be able to relate to others. *"It is not good that man should be alone; I will make him a helper fit for him"* (Genesis 2:16). This statement from God leads to the creation of Eve and highlights that God saw that humans need to be with others.

As a teenager I found this idea of linking with other people rather difficult. I kept my distance from others because if they asked me about my family I felt tears welling up. But when I went to the university student's hostel I started to make strong friendships with the other students whose families were in other countries. This helped me to feel safe and I learnt about my new "family", their religions and their ethnic and national identities. This helped me to decide to be an Australian and I went to the Court and declared myself to be an "Australian citizen". My identity was now taking root.

> Linking to others can be difficult

So part of being a person is developing a social identity. This usually means we see ourselves as belonging to a social group. Whatever group this is will mean that we have noted certain categories of the group and we identify ourselves as having some similar features. In an attempt to assimilate with the group we may find our personal identity being strongly influenced by our membership in the group. This could happen in the context of our community which may have a strong sense of its social structure, such as the Amish community in the USA, or a local youth gang, or members of a religious sect.

We either behave according to the strictures of the community and adapt our self-image to the community expectations or leave. By leaving we lose our support structures and this can have an impact on our self-image. I saw this happen when a teenage friend decided to leave his Hindu connections to become a Christian. He lost his family and his Hindu friends and had to find a new group of friends in the Christian community.

As a member of a family we may at some stage choose to leave the family home and live elsewhere. Until then the family will have some influence on values and identity and may have some influence also on expectations. Whatever the social groups are to which we belong they will:

* cause us to build relationships and, in doing so,
* enable us to choose and develop our values, and
* cause us to consider our emotions as we work out how to respond to friendships, to emotional events and to messages communicated to us.

Belonging to others and developing our values will impact our self-image and thus help us to understand and perhaps change aspects of our own identity.

In some countries the dominant religion may require all people living in that country to be members of the official national religion. Those who choose not to be part of that religious group will be treated as unacceptable and this may result in social sanctions (such as imprisonment or rejection by neighbours). This social identity has a significant impact on each person. It robs the individual of the freedom to choose. It forces the person to have an identity which is not accepted by others. Examples of this are found in those Islamic communities which demand that everyone born in the country is a Muslim or else treated as *dhimmis* (second class citizens with many restrictions). In India the Shiv Sena and the Vishwa Hindu Parishad societies regard all Indians as being Hindus and all others

> Our religious or other friendships will impact our behaviour and our identity

are liable to persecution. This is a desire to declare nationalism in terms of religion. Religious nationalism is oppressive and a source of confusion for the identity of citizens. In the first three centuries of the western era, citizens of Roman-controlled countries were expected to declare Caesar as Lord, and failure to do so could result in persecution. One's social identity was then, and is still in the world today, a matter of public concern.

A similar situation occurs wherever a political ideology is regarded as the supreme ideology and one which all must follow.[7] These social identities rob us of the capacity to determine for ourselves our values, faith and the meaning we give to events. It thus limits the development of our identities. Some have argued that these social identities impact our unconscious mind and thus generate in us some behaviour patterns which we may dislike. Others would argue that we are being "brain-washed" by these intrusive social identities. Certainly the social identity required of us in some places means that we are seeking to be identified with the local culture and thus within our own identity we are divided. This situation requires of us an exercise in reconstructing our own identity by determining exactly where we stand in respect to the social identity, the differences we will live with and what punishment we are willing to endure.

Recreating our social self-image

Most of us are thrust into different social settings and we may choose to identify ourselves according to the relationships we are pursuing at any one point of time. This means that we allow our relationships to determine our projected image and this could mean a change even in our beliefs and values. To the extent we allow others to cause us to change our self-image, we are reconstructing our image.

---

7   This includes North Korea, Laos and the northern part of Vietnam.

Living with students from many Asian countries enabled me to regard myself as part of their world and I spent one of my university vacations living in Asia with the families of these students. This strengthened my determination to oppose those who were antagonistic to people of other nations. It also helped me see myself as a person who belonged to the world and not just to Australia.

Changes are usually in response to the comments and behaviours of those who have some influence on us. We so often want people to see us in an acceptable way and so we project an acceptable image. Some years ago while studying in Chicago I spent a day with a street gang and discovered how a new teenage resident in the street was willing to go and kill a passer-by. This boy wanted to be seen to be like the others in the gang by being willing to kill. Clearly there is danger in this approach as it can mean that we are willing to continue to re-form our projected image in the light of changing relationships. Our projected image becomes our self-image after we have had time to eliminate blurring of edges between our view of our self and our projected image. Sadly this self-image becomes dependent on our relationships.

> Allowing others to influence us can take us down an unhelpful track!

We can see how this happens when certain roles force on us a given pattern of behaviour determined by the exercise of that role in the community. For instance, a police person acts with authority as a police person, but in the home this person may be non-authoritative. If this person acts authoritatively in the home then there is a blurring between the work role and the home role, and we have a problem in that the person is failing to reflect adequately on him/herself in determining what is the essence of his/her personality and what is appropriate in each setting. This is the issue of substance and style, of identity and role. The person's style may change in different relationships and the expression of this in different roles. But who the person really is — what we referred to in chapter 2 as the substantial nature of the person — does not necessarily change. Yet when the boundary between substance and style becomes blurred, the social relationships usually deteriorate.

By the way, I was able to get some of the street gang, who I refer to above, to come with me to a local Christian organisation which works with street gangs to help the boys to see themselves as important, without needing to kill anyone just to gain acceptance.

Loss of face

In some societies a refusal can mean a "loss of face" for the individual. One's "face" is considered to be the prominent personal factor in being who we are in the community. It reflects our social self. Our "face" identifies the quality of our relationship with others. Refusal in some cultures means that the person is of little value and has lost whatever social status had been attributed to that person. The common way around this is to prevent loss of face by saying "yes" to the request, even if not intending to act on it. There can be loss of face when one rejects a possible marriage partner. Loss of face can also occur by not agreeing to be involved in a religious ritual. In these ways the idea of a loss of face is a mechanism for social control in the community and in the family. In most significant circumstances it is hard to avoid this loss as the community makes certain expectations of its members. It may mean changing and becoming a member of a different social group. It will mean accepting some loss of self-esteem. We need to decide the issues for which we are prepared to suffer. This decision is itself a direct reflection of our identity and the self-image we want to project. This is and should be our own choice.

Questions for reflection and discussion

→ Identify the relationships that are important to you.
→ How do each of these relationships contribute to your sense of identity?

Chapter 9

Our Soul, Spirit and Body

We are whole people. Each one of us is unique. Each one of us can relate to our Creator both while we are on earth and in heaven. There is a range of terms that can help us understand this.

We have a unique presence on earth

There is often confusion over the terms, soul, spirit and body. The words "spirit" and "soul" are generally used interchangeably in the Bible. Both refer to the fact that God created us with a personal identity which enables us to relate to him. God is Spirit and his image is constituted in our spirit/soul: this is our own personal centre for reflection and the means by which we can connect with God. What is clear is that we are whole people. We are not made up of parts which can be distinguished. We do not *have* a spirit/soul, but rather we *are* spirit/soul. We do not *have* a body, we *are* a body. Since we are whole people, both a body and a soul/spirit, we have a unique presence on earth, the capacity to be in a relationship with our Creator and we can look forward also to being with our Creator after our bodily death.

When, as a small boy, I visited the army hospital for wounded Indian soldiers, I found some of them wondering what would happen after death. They told me, as Hindu believers, that by being good soldiers they would not be reincarnated as other Hindus would, but would end up in Nirvana. They explained that this would be "like being a drop of water in the ocean". I asked about their body and they said that this would be burnt, it was just their spirit which would go on existing, but be lost in the mass of nothingness. I was too young to understand all this so I asked Lora who explained to me the Hindu ideas about death. Even then as a child it was a comfort for me to know that, as a Christian, I mattered to God and would be with him and not be lost in the nothingness of Nirvana.

In my student days I was living with some Indian students and found myself discussing what the soul was and what we would look like in heaven. I turned to the Bible and in reading Genesis 2:7 I saw that the word "soul"[8] is based on the Hebrew word for "life". So this passage reads:

> *The Lord God formed man of the dust of the ground, and breathed into his nostrils the breath of life; and man became a living soul (nepesh).*

(see footnote below; this passage is from the Hebrew Bible, Genesis 2:7).

This means that Adam became a living being when he was created (*"of the dust of the ground"*) *and* God breathed into him. Because God gave Adam *"the breath of life"*, Adam became a living person, a soul *(nepesh)* having both body and the breath of life.

Body, soul and spirit

The word "soul" *(nepesh)* generally refers to "me" or "myself". For instance, *"My soul has thirsted for you…"* (Psalm 63:1), or *"My soul longs, yes, faints for the courts of the Lord…"* (Psalm 84:2).

In these Old Testament texts, "soul" essentially means "me" or "I" (although the Hebrew word can have some additional meaning). Likewise in the New Testament, the word "soul"[9] can refer to "me". For example:

> *I will say to my soul, "Soul, you have ample goods laid up for many years…" but God said to him, "Fool! This night your soul is required of you…"* (Luke 12:19–20)

---

8 In the Hebrew Old Testament "soul" is *nepesh*.
9 "Soul" in the NT is *psyche*.

So "soul" is referring to the living person, to "me". Paul sometimes uses the word "body" instead of "soul", but he is still referring to the soul/body, namely to "me". Thus in 1 Corinthians 15, referring to the resurrection of the dead, Paul states:

> *It is sown a natural body [10] (i.e. a soul/body) it is raised a spiritual body.[11] (1 Cor. 15:44)*

We also find in the Bible another term for ourselves, namely, "spirit". The word, "spirit"[12] is sometimes used in reference to the action of relating to God. For example in the Old Testament:

> *Create in me a clean heart, O God, and renew a right spirit (ruach) within me. (Psalm 51:10)*

Here the Psalmist is referring to himself as a person, indeed as a sinner. He is not saying "one part of me has sinned", but rather that "I have sinned, so please in your steadfast love forgive me and create in me a new person".

Likewise in the New Testament, the same use of the word "spirit"[13] appears:

> *God is spirit (pneuma) and those who worship him must worship in spirit (pneuma) and truth. (John 4:24)*

We are a spirit because God is Spirit and he has breathed into us life/spirit, so we communicate with God the Holy Spirit through our spirit. We can now see that we are enabled to worship God because he has created us with a soul/spirit. Isaiah 42:5 states:

> *thus says God, the Lord, ...who spread out the earth and what comes from it, who gives breath to the people on it and spirit to those who walk in it.*

---

10 "Natural body", *soma psychikon*, based on the Greek word for physical life.
11 "Spiritual body", *soma pneumatikon*, based on the Greek word *pneuma*, for *spirit*.
12 "Spirit" is *ruach* in the OT and *pneuma* (Greek) in the NT.
13 Again this is the word *pneuma* for "Spirit" which in Hebrew would be *ruach*.

Another example:

> *For who knows a person's thoughts except the spirit (pneuma) of that person which is in him. (1 Corinthians 2:11)*

Now we can see that both "soul" and "spirit" refer to the self, although the word "spirit" is also used to refer to our ability to communicate with God who is Spirit, whereas "soul" refers to our identity and God's image in us. We have been gifted with our soul/spirit by God so that we can be in fellowship with him. So when I refer to "me" I mean my body/soul/spirit. We cannot separate these dimensions of ourselves. Our unique identity is always "me" on earth and also with Christ after death.

Paul's use of the terms "spirit", "soul" and "body" in 1 Thessalonians 5:23 has been debated by scholars because he uses these words altogether in the one statement:

> *Now may the God of peace sanctify you completely and may your whole spirit (pneuma) and soul (psyche) and body (soma) be kept blameless at the coming of our Lord Jesus Christ.*

There is some difficulty in working out what Paul is saying in this passage, but it can be resolved when we realise that the opening phrase states that God may sanctify us "completely and entirely" and so Paul is referring to the whole person. By using the words "spirit", "soul" and "body", Paul wants the church to know that we are to be wholly sanctified to the Lord.

Paul may have also had in mind that the Christians in Thessalonica could have been influenced by fourth-century BC Greek philosophers. Thinkers like Plato considered that the earthly body was quite separate from the soul (the inner self) and spirit (human connection with the divine). Paul wants to declare that we are unique individuals made up of an immortal spirit *(pneuma)* — or what may be called our immortal soul *(psyche)* — through which we are in contact with God, and we have a mortal body *(soma)*. Although Paul uses two separate words — soul and spirit — he is referring to the identity of the whole person, an identity which is complete on earth when we include the word "body". James makes this clear in his statement in 2:26 that *"the body without the spirit (pneumatos) is dead".*

Our mortal body is formed out of the dust (Genesis 2:7) and is shed at the point of death, but our personal identity, our soul/spirit, is immortal. Hence Paul declares:

> "Soul" and "Spirit" both refer to our identity

> *So it is with the resurrection of the dead. What is sown is perishable, what is raised is imperishable. It is sown in dishonour, it is raised in glory. It is sown in weakness; it is raised in power. It is sown a natural body; it is raised a spiritual body (pneumatikon). (1 Corinthians 15:42–44)*

This continuing identity, this spirit/soul, is a gift from God. He created us to be a personal being, a unity, a single identity made in his image, and so each one of us has continuity as a person. Furthermore, because we are made in the image of God, that is because we have a spirit/soul, we have the capacity to converse with God through his written word and the Holy Spirit.

God created each one of us as a whole person (spiritual and physical) so that we could both walk this earth and be in a relationship with him, just as Jesus walked this earth and yet was always in a relationship with his Father.

The word "spirit" *(pneuma)* is regarded by Paul as the same as "soul" *(psyche)*. There are many different views among scholars about these two words, but the Reformation position seems to be that Paul wanted to cover all aspects of our lives regardless of our philosophical understanding and that we are actually made up of two parts, namely our soul/spirit (the spiritual dimension) and our body (the physical dimension). God made our bodies out of the ground and hence our bodies will die and return to the ground, but God breathed into Adam (Genesis 2:7) and hence God's breath enables Adam to be "a living soul" *(pneuma)* as stated by Paul in 1 Corinthians 15:45. It is this living being, this spirit/soul which is immortal and which will go to be with God at the point of death in his heaven.

The question which then arises is *can I be identified when I go to heaven?* What does my identity consist of? Will I be raised a spiritual body *(pneumatikon,* see this Greek word above) with my personal uniqueness and will I be recognisable (read 1 Corinthians15:42–58)? What we do not know is what our heavenly, recreated body will "look" like. Even the word "look" assumes a bodily function, but we do not know how we will recognise each other in heaven. As a new spiritual body we may not have the "mass" of our earthly body, but we will be recognised, the attributes of our personality and what makes each one of us unique will be evident, just as they were when Jesus' resurrected body was eventually recognised by the disciples (John 20:14–29 and see 1 Corinthians 15:12–22).

Our essential, eternal identity

There is much we do not understand, but what we do know is that when God created humankind he *"breathed into the nostrils the breath of life and man* [=humankind] *became a living soul" (nepesh)* (Genesis 2:7).

The Psalmist declares:

> *Into your hand I commit my spirit (ruach); you have redeemed me, O Lord, faithful God. (Psalm 31:5)*

This is strengthened by Ecclesiastes 12:7 which states,

> *the dust returns to the ground from which it came and the spirit (ruach) returns to God who gave it.*

This passage makes clear that the body and the soul/spirit are made of different features. The one can decompose and the other cannot be dissolved.

Thus the term "soul/spirit" can be used to refer to that part of our identity which is essential to who we are without referring to our racial inheritance and physical features, which can be referred to as our "static" features. God did not plan our existence with a view to a complete and final decomposition. As his perfect creation he has given us the capacity to choose to belong to him forever or not to so belong (this is in response to God's grace, 1 John 5:12). By belonging to him forever, our uniqueness continues and we will always belong to his kingdom (1 Corinthians 15:50–58).

Our creation

The fact that God creates us as humans via the process he put in place, namely, human procreation, doesn't diminish the fact that he is involved in that procreation process and that he *"forms the spirit in human beings"* (Zechariah 12:1 TNIV). The fact that God determined to enable humankind to procreate highlights that procreation is a result of overall creation activity.

At the same time God creates us within the natural process of gestation and birth and since we are made in his image we are the one unique person. This continuity may be called a *spirit*, as in the Ecclesiastes passage above, or referred to as a *soul* (Job 10:8–12; Psalm 139:13–16). When we refer to a person, usually by name, we are referring to the whole person (by implication we are referring to the body and soul/spirit). When we do refer to an individual person we are highlighting that person's uniqueness.

The soul/spirit is created by God as our link with him. We are a whole person and God has created us, body and soul/spirit. The importance of our body is indicated by the statement that the Holy Spirit chooses to be alive in us:

> *Do you not know that your body is the temple of the Holy Spirit within you, whom you have from God? You are not your own, for you were bought with a price. So glorify God in your body. (1 Corinthians 6:19)*

We will be changed

Paul refers to the *"redemption of our bodies"* (in Romans 8:23; see also 1 Corinthians 15:35–43). It is not just our souls, but the whole person which is being redeemed. We cannot fully understand how God has created us as whole persons reflecting his image and having continuity (Romans 2:7), but we accept this as truth revealed in the Scriptures. Since nothing is impossible for God, he created us out of nothing and he can recreate us for entry into his heaven as the same persons we were on earth, yet unable to sin again (1 Corinthians 15:52: *"the dead will be raised imperishable, and we shall be changed"*). We will be raised a spiritual body (see the full text above).

> We cannot fully understand how God created us, but we do reflect his image

We have limited knowledge about this, but we do know that we will be totally filled with giving God our praise. We do know that our heavenly body will be perfect, as everything in heaven will be perfect.

We also know that Jesus promises a resurrected life for all who believe in him:

> *I am the resurrection and the life. Anyone who believes in me will live, even though they die, and whoever lives by believing in me will never die. (John 11:25–26)*

The resurrection is as complex and as wonderful as the act of creation!

Our human body does matter to God

Let us dig a little deeper! The body is very important in the Scriptures. Jesus was incarnated (John 1:14). Hence, the fact he was willing to enter the world in "the flesh" is in itself a reminder as to how important it was that Jesus and the Father recognised the physical body. Jesus offered his body as the supreme sacrifice on the cross. He was crucified, but he was raised again from the dead. Jesus gave up his spirit to the Father when he announced *"it is finished"* (John19:30). We can understand that *"the body without the spirit is dead"* (James 2:26). When Jesus was raised from the dead his spirit and his resurrected body with his additional powers were again as one. Although the two people on the Emmaus Road did not initially recognise Jesus, nevertheless they, and later the disciples, did recognise him. It was the same body, the same person, the same identity who was raised from the dead (see Luke 24:39). In our case we will shed our earthly body, but we will be given by God our new heavenly body which will be without the pain of sin or of suffering (Revelation 21:4 and see Philippians 3:20–21). So we will recognise each other in the ideal form in which we were created, just as the disciples recognised Moses and Elijah talking with Jesus (Matthew 17:3).

We are one person consisting of body/soul/spirit and our identity will continue to be essential to our resurrected body. Our identity will remain the same. We are unique just as our DNA[14] is unique and although we change as we grow up and continue to grow, nevertheless God knows who we are and our identity is maintained. Stephen clearly understood this as he prayed when he was being stoned, *"Lord Jesus receive my spirit"* (in other words, "receive me", Acts 7:59).

> Jesus was the same person with the same identity when he was met with after his resurrection

What a joy it will be to be in God's daily presence and to see ourselves as

---

[14] DNA, or deoxyribonucleic acid, is the hereditary material in humans and almost all other organisms.

sinless, perfect beings, identifiable to all who know us. So in answer to the question posed at the beginning of this chapter, what will we consist of in the resurrection body — we will be a transformed person with our own spirit/soul and a new imperishable body. This is summed up in those striking words of Paul:

> *If then you have been raised with Christ, seek the things that are above, where Christ is seated at the right hand of God. Set your mind on things that are above, not on things that are on the earth. For you have died, and your life is hidden with Christ in God. When Christ who is your life appears, then you also will appear with him in glory. (Colossians 3:3–4)*

Questions for reflection and discussion

- → Be encouraged by a view of heaven expressed in 2 Corinthians 4:17 and 5:1.
- → What aspects of heaven do we see 1 Peter1:3-5?
- → In what ways do you think your soul/spirit can be nourished?

Chapter 10

If I Think I Am a Failure

Failures do not determine our identity. Failures are stepping stones not stumbling blocks. God will enable us to find another way forward.

Responding to failure

When I arrived in Egypt I was sent to a local school where the teaching was in Arabic. Egyptian Arabic sounds a little different from Palestinian Arabic so I was battling to understand it and then the teacher told us to write down what he had just said in Arabic and I couldn't write Arabic! I was a failure and asked the missionaries I was staying with to allow me not to go to school. I enjoyed the fun I had after I left school as I wandered around the market and the missionary hospital where the missionaries worked, but without language I couldn't talk to anyone and was very conscious of my inadequacy.

Looking back I can see that my identity could have been thoroughly undermined by thinking that I was of no use. However, later experiences in Australia helped me to think this through more clearly. I discovered that some people were unable to get work and had lost confidence because of this. Then at my Australian high school I became aware of how shattered some students were when they failed to get into a top sporting team. As I have thought about this I realised that the first important point to grasp is that failing in some application or activity means only that we did not gain access to that activity. We may have a long list of failures and lost opportunities, or think that we have been a failure in school or in our home, but all this does not mean that we personally are a failure!

> **Failure can be a stepping stone**

It can be a help to look at those, from a human point of view, who seem to have failed, but who have not allowed that failure to become a stumbling block. Instead they have used each failure as a stepping stone to move on. One such person is a man who had only 18 months of school, his business failed him, the girl he loved died and he subsequently suffered from depression. He stood for election to the USA Senate and was defeated, but in 1860 he was elected as President of the USA. He was Abraham Lincoln. Although he had a number of failures, we remember him only by his one success.[15]

Another example of failure was Pierre Curie who, after 487 unsuccessful attempts at an experiment, said to his wife "It cannot be done". Madame Curie said, "It will be done".[16] The world has ever since acclaimed their work in discovering radio-active elements, such as polonium and radium, without knowing the determination needed in the face of apparent defeat.

On the missionary front there have been many failures by applicants. One of these was Gladys Aylward. She was told that she was not educated enough to be sent as a missionary. So she continued to scrub floors until she had enough to pay her boat fare to China and there among her many activities she saved the lives of hundreds of children during the Japanese invasion. Her story is told in a book entitled, *Small Woman*.[17] The person who rescued me as an orphan in Palestine had been told by her missionary society that, although she had worked with them for 15 years, they would not continue their support. She nevertheless paid her own way to Palestine — read the story in *Never Alone*.[18]

---

15   William E. Gienapp, *Abraham Lincoln and Civil War America: A Biography*, (New York: Oxford University Press, 2002).
16   *Nobel Lectures: Physics 1901–21* (Amsterdam: Elsevier Publishing Co., 1967).
17   These stories are recorded in Robyn Claydon, *Me a Success? Living Skills for Teenagers* (ANZEA Publishers, 1989).
18   Cecily Paterson, *Never Alone*, (Adelaide: SPCKA, 2006).

Some strategies

How can we build some strategies for responding to a failure in our own lives? Here are some suggestions:

The *first* is not to make failures determine our identity and think of ourselves as a failure.

The *second* is to use every failure as a stepping stone not a stumbling bock. There may be a good reason for our failure in a relationship or in securing a job. What we need to do is to examine the situation with a critical mind and decide in what ways we may need to change our behaviour or how we should present ourselves. We should not blame the other person, but determine what can be learnt from the failure and use this as a stepping stone for our own development.

The *third* is to realise afresh that there can be certainty in our lives. The most important fact is what Jesus has done for us. There is real certainty about this as explained in the Bible, particularly in passages such as John 3:16–18, Romans 8, 1 Corinthians 15, and Ephesians 3. Our salvation (2 Corinthians 1:10 and 1 Thessalonians 5:8) is definite and is evidenced in Christ's work on the cross and his resurrection. We are assured of this because of God's grace towards us (2 Thessalonians 2:16–17) and his love for us (Ephesians 1:18). While our "hope" in Jesus is the unique certainty that he welcomes us into his family for ever, yet we can still have other hopes such as the emotional support of our close friends and often our family. It is very helpful to have some friends who are our prayer partners. If we cannot think of people to fill this role, then we could join a Bible study home group and invite the other members to pray for us as we pray for them.

The *fourth* strategy is to consult another person who may have some expertise in the area of concern or who could mentor us as we continue to think through the different ways in which we could move ahead. The mentor doesn't advise, but listens to us and prays with us and thus enables us to be transparent about ourselves in this particular aspect of our lives.

This transparency enables us to see our identity as we truly are and not put ourselves down by a failure.

The *fifth* strategy can be to take hold of some verses from the Scriptures and realise that God does care about us and enables us to recover and find another way forward. Read Hebrews 12:12 — *"Lift up your tired hands, strengthen your trembling knees".* Or see Isaiah 40:29 — *"He strengthens those who are weak and tired".* Another helpful text is 1 Peter 5:7 — *"Leave all your worries with him, for he cares for you".*

As we pray, seeking to find out what the next step could be, we can be encouraged by this verse in Psalm 33:18, 20–22.

> *But the eyes of the Lord are on those who fear him, on those whose hope is in his unfailing love… we wait in hope for the Lord; he is our help and shield. In him our hearts rejoice for we trust in his holy name. May your unfailing love rest upon us, O Lord, even as we put our hope in you.*

May the God of hope fill you with all joy and peace as you trust in him so you may overflow with hope, knowing that your identity need not be diminished by failures, but is strengthened by bringing you even closer to the Lord (see Romans 15:13).

Questions for reflection and discussion

- → Can you think of examples in your life of situations where not being successful in something has been an incentive to try harder or perhaps move in a different direction?
- → To what extent can God or other people help you in this?

Chapter 11

God's Identity

We know that there is one Divine Being whom we call God. We know about him because he has revealed himself in history and through Jesus Christ. We know about him because of his grace and love.

Historical evidence that God exists

My wife and I enjoy reading about and visiting archaeological sites in the Middle East. As you walk the streets in the old city of Jerusalem, or look at a possible tomb where Jesus' body was laid for three days, you will find that there is an amazing connection between the biblical record about Jesus and what you will find. One of the arguments we hear from some non-Christians is that there is no archaeological evidence that God exists. No-one has seen God, yet we do have the evidence that God has revealed enough about himself for us to be able to gain some understanding of who he is, what his purposes are and how he relates to us. God has revealed his identity through his actions with the children of Israel (Joshua 1:9; 3:5; 24:15). This is further evidenced by the prophecies in the history of the children of Israel coming true and hence making it clear that God is a communicating God and his word will come into being (for instance, Exodus 12–13, Deuteronomy 33, Isaiah 40). Then we also have the realisation of the

> God revealed himself to the children of Israel through his promises being realised

prophecy of the coming of the messiah and Jesus' actual presence on earth and his saving work. Jesus the Son of God took on human flesh and intersected with our history (Hebrews 1:1–3).

For some, God is perceived as hiding himself. Some would wish that knowing God would not be an act of faith, but that we could personally meet Jesus and so know for sure that he exists and he created us. It is interesting that many people who did meet Jesus when he walked this earth did not believe that he was the Son of God. Even his disciples had trouble identifying him as the Messiah and Saviour until his resurrection and ascension. However, the Father, Son and Holy Spirit have revealed themselves to us in ways which are adequate for us to grasp these truths and respond. The writer to the young Christian community stated in very clear terms:

> *Long ago, at many times and in many ways, God spoke to our fathers by the prophets, but in these last days he has spoken to us by his Son, whom he appointed the heir of all things, through whom also he created the world. He is the radiance of the glory of God and the exact imprint of his nature, and he upholds the universe by the word of his power. After making purification for sins, he sat down at the right hand of the Majesty on high. (Hebrews 1:1–3)*

This passage states many points about who Jesus is. The writer continues in the letter to the Hebrews to remake or to extend the points, in case the readers do not grasp all that is being said. For instance in 2:9, *"we see Jesus… crowned with glory and honour because of the suffering of death"* and in 4:14, *"since then we have a great high priest who has passed through the heavens, Jesus the Son of God, let us hold fast our confession"*. These passages in Hebrews point to the forgiving nature of God and so the grace we can access in Jesus Christ. Grace is God's gift to us and refers to his forgiveness and his loving call to us to belong to his kingdom.

We can understand that our knowledge of what Jesus did when he intersected with our history was previously revealed by the prophets of old and their words were recorded in the Old Testament (OT). These prophetic words were proven to be true by Jesus coming into our world through birth, through his teaching and his miracles, and finally through his crucifixion, resurrection and ascension.

Father, Son and Holy Spirit

There are some hidden facts about Jesus. For instance we have difficulty describing his unique relationship within the Godhead, but we know that the Scriptures declare Jesus to be the Son of God (see Matthew 3:17; 28:18–20; John 1; Hebrews 1) and that this triune single Godhead consists of the Father, the Son and the Holy Spirit.[19] It is in fact the joint activity and the love within the Godhead which demonstrate that God can and does show his love towards us. He does so not because he needs us as a basis of giving and of gaining love, but because he is love (1 John 4:8; Ephesians 3:19) and wants to demonstrate his love to us.

Our mind can go back to the OT where we read about God revealing himself to Moses. We do not know what Moses knew before the occasion when he was in the Midian desert near Mt Horeb. He probably knew that there

> God did make himself known to Moses

was a God as he had learnt something about God which had been passed down through the generations (Exodus 2). On this occasion he was amazed at the scene of a burning bush. Moses learnt from this encounter that there is a God. The very existence of God who came to Moses highlights both the incredible importance of God's existence and also the wonderful fact that Moses did not have to find God or to imagine that there may be a divine

---

[19] The briefest of the many books on the Trinity is Royce G. Gruenler, *The Trinity in the Gospel of John*, (Eugene, OR: Wipf & Stock, 1986).. Another is William J. La Due, *The Trinity Guide to the Trinity*, (Harrisburg: Trinity Press, 2003).

being. God came to him. By stating *"I am the God of your father, the God of Abraham, the God of Isaac, and the God of Jacob"* (Exodus 3:6), God is revealing his identity historically and with Moses himself as well as with the children of Israel (v.7).

"I am" in the OT and in the NT

As the conversation continues, Moses demands to know how he can report to the Israelites that he has been told to lead them and who has sent him. God's response is *"**I am** [YHWH] who **I am**"*. And God said, *"Say to the people of Israel, **I am** has sent me to you"* (Exodus 3:14). Then comes the outstanding statement: *"Say this to the people of Israel, 'The Lord the God of your fathers, the God of Abraham, the God of Isaac and the God of Jacob has sent me to you. This is my name forever, and thus I am to be remembered throughout all generations'"* (v.15).

Moses now has a clear picture. He knows who God is and can refer to him personally and declare that God will be with the Israelites from generation to generation. This in itself is a wonderful fact that God is a personal God. As Moses reveals later and is recorded in the OT book of the Exodus, God created humankind and talked with them personally. He cares about the Israelites and is caring for them personally. He came and talked to Moses personally and so this God who has revealed himself as a personal God wants to be personally in touch with each one of us also. God's statement to Moses reveals his power, his eternal presence and his character. This God who covenanted with Abraham, Isaac and Jacob is the covenanting YHWH (the Hebrew word for "I am") and this history indicates that God will continue to relate to the Israelites and us today. His covenanted (defined) relationship is everlasting (see Hebrews 8). The message of continuity about YHWH, who is forever, is an important theme. We find this reference to God throughout the OT; and in Isaiah 48:12 we see the importance of the challenge to Israel, *"**I am** the first and **I am** the last"*. In other words YHWH is the true living God who is at the beginning and at the end of all things.

The New Testament connects the *"I am"* statements with Jesus. So the *"I am"* statement used by God (YHWH) when talking to Moses is used by Jesus as reported in John's Gospel such as:

> *Jesus said to them, "**I am** the bread of life" (John 6:36), and*

> *Jesus said to them, Truly, truly I say to you, before Abraham was **I am**". (John 8:58)*[20]

There is a continuity of God's presence on earth in Jesus and this helps to highlight the trinitarian nature of the Godhead (namely that God is Father, Son and Holy Spirit). As God has created us as spirit we can start to understand that central to our identity is our capacity to communicate with the triune God.

In fact humans find the *ultimate goal of their identity* in being able to communicate with their Creator. It is for this reason that Jesus explained to the disciples that:

> *"I will not leave you as orphans; I will come to you… On that day you will realize that I am in my Father, and you are in me, and I am in you… Whoever has my commands and keeps them…I will love them and show myself to them… Remain in me as I also remain in you". (John 14:18–21 and 15:4 TNIV)*

Our God has been revealed through Moses and the words of the prophets of old and in Jesus. He is the self-named God who is eternal and calls us to live with him eternally.

---

20 See also John 8:12; 10:7–14, 11:25; 14:6; 15:1–2.

Questions for reflection or discussion

→ If you were asked to write down the characteristics of God's identity what would you note?

→ List some ways in which you can connect with God.

→ How would you answer someone who says there is no proof of the existence of God?

Chapter 12

Being in Christ — Part 1

*Being in Christ means allowing Jesus
to mould us.*

Our identity is not in a vacuum

Leading camps in the Pacific Islands helped me to realise that the commonly used phrase "Christ in us" just didn't make sense no matter what language it was translated into. So I had to think, "what does the Bible mean when it refers to Christians being 'in Christ Jesus?'" (2 Corinthians 5:17; Galatians 2:20).

> We have been created so as to be able to build a relationship with our Creator — this is a unique human capacity

For a start it means that God created us in his image so that we would be endowed with the capacity to be in a living relationship with him. This is possible through the work of Jesus Christ who has forgiven us and made it possible for the original purpose of creation to be rediscovered in us today. Just as Adam and Eve were in communication with God, so we too can be in communication with God who has disclosed himself in Jesus. By accepting Jesus' forgiveness and investing our lives in him we become what Paul calls "a new creation": *So if anyone is in Christ, there is a new creation"* (2 Corinthians 5:17 NRSV). I found this helpful in a small way, but this gave rise to a further question from the campers as to how I can become a new creation?

I focused in one of my camp talks on the ultimate expression of God's intention that we be bearers of his image. All humans are created with the "substantial" and "functional" presence of God's image (see chapter 2), but the "relational" presence is only a possibility when each of us accepts Jesus as central to our lives and then the relational presence is fulfilled. I explained to the campers that having accepted Jesus as personal Lord and Saviour we become *"joint heirs with Jesus"*, part of God's family (Romans 8:17). This completion of being created *"in the image of God"* means that we can call God "our Father" (Matthew 6:9 *"Our Father in heaven…"*)

Having understood that our identity is based on God's creative work, I then explained that we are not really on our own, Christ is with us at all times so our identity does not exist in a vacuum. The first step is to be identified with Christ. For this reason Paul wrote to the Galatian Christians and stated:

> *I have been crucified with Christ. It is no longer I who live, but Christ who lives in me. (Galatians 2:20)*

By being identified with Christ we will recognise changes which need to be made and we can ask God the Holy Spirit to help us to make these changes: *"We walk not according to the flesh but according to the Spirit"* (Romans 8:1–11).

Our life is now centred in Christ, but transformation is a slow process! It comes about as we read the Scriptures and seek to be obedient. The New Testament declares God's desire:

> **Transformation is a slow process**

> *I will put my laws into their minds and write them on their hearts, and I will be their God and they shall be my people. (Hebrews 8:10)*

This statement is referred to as "a covenant" and means we have a *defined relationship* with God. God has called us to be in a relationship with him and he has defined the basis for this relationship. Since we want to be in relationship with God we are obedient to him because our faith in God is growing. This relationship is possible because part of God's image is in us and we can therefore communicate with him and he with us. This is the spiritual dimension to ourselves from the Christian viewpoint.

One evidence of this spirituality is shown by the way most communities seek to find the divine. For Christians, who God is becomes clear through the prophets of old and in Jesus. So we know who he is. It is this spiritual dimension in us which is enlivened by the work of the Holy Spirit in us. So Paul states:

> *…if the Spirit of him who raised Jesus from the dead dwells in you he…will also give life to your mortal bodies through his Spirit who dwells in you. (Romans 8:11)*

Our faith comes from our commitment to Jesus our Lord and Saviour. It is a statement of faith that the Holy Spirit is at work in us.

> **Our faith will continue to grow as we see God at work in our lives**

This is strengthened by the awareness of all that God has done in creation and through his written word (Hebrews 1:1–2). Our faith will continue to grow as we see God at work in our lives through answered prayer and through seeing ourselves being transformed and becoming more Christ-like in our behaviour.

We have noted already that we are created in the image of God and that we are in a defined relationship with God. God has made himself known, but he can still seem rather remote. The Scriptures make it clear that our relationship with God is defined by a personal relationship with Jesus Christ. This personal relationship is taken hold of at the very moment we decide to accept Christ's free gift of salvation. What Jesus did on the cross was to take upon himself the penalty for our rebelliousness. This rebelliousness or what is called "sin" is a way of summing up that we have treated God as if he didn't matter. Alternatively, we may have regarded some religious character or other object in our lives as central to who we are. Christ, in his mercy, has offered to forgive us for this, at no cost to us. So when we accept Christ's free gift we are then in a permanent relationship with God. This relationship is expressed through our faith in Jesus. He is the "mediator", the one and only person who connects us to his Father. This was made clear to the early NT church:

> *For there is one God, and one mediator between God and human beings, Christ Jesus, himself human, who gave himself as a ransom for all people. (1 Timothy 2:5 TNIV)*

In Paul's letter to the Christians in Rome, he says:

> *You, however, are not in the flesh but in the Spirit, if in fact the Spirit of God dwells in you. Anyone who does not have the Spirit of Christ does not belong to him. But if Christ is in you, although the body is dead because of sin, the Spirit is life because of righteousness. If the Spirit of him who raised Jesus from the dead dwells in you, he who raised Christ Jesus from the dead will also give life to your mortal bodies through his Spirit who dwells in you. (Romans 8:9–11)*

This text needs some explanation!

Firstly, Paul refers both to the Holy Spirit and to Jesus Christ. He is not blurring the distinction between Jesus and the Holy Spirit, rather he is pointing to the intimate relationship between them. This relationship is indissoluble. So being created in the image of God, and having Jesus and the Holy Spirit in us, we realise that the Trinity is real and is at work in us. This means that through the presence of the Holy Spirit we have a new life, a life changed by Christ's work on the cross, and we have a guarantee of our

> **The Holy Spirit wants to be at work in us**

new and permanent status as members of God's kingdom (see more about the kingdom in 5b in the next chapter). So Paul makes clear to the Corinthian Christians that:

> *He who has prepared us for this very thing is God, and has given us the Spirit as a guarantee. (2 Corinthians 5:5)*

The Holy Spirit, referred to in the Romans text above, is both the Spirit of God and the Spirit of Christ and this is evidence of the triune God. It is God the Holy Spirit who is given to us as a guarantee that we belong to Jesus, and as an indicator that he is the one who is responding to our request to be transformed and made to be increasingly Christ-like.

Secondly, Paul tells the Romans *"Christ is in you..."*. The ways in which Christ is in us are explained below.

Our identity will be moulded

I found I needed to explore this more fully with the campers. So I outlined that we can develop our identity as we allow our relationship with Christ to mould us, since he is "in" us. The triune God is in us in the following ways:

(1) The reality of *being created in the image of God* starts to make more sense when we apply the fact that the perfect representation of God is Jesus (Hebrews 1 and 2; Corinthians 4:4; Colossians 1:15). Jesus did actually walk this earth; he actually demonstrated his love for each one of us through his crucifixion and resurrection; and he is at work in us moulding and shaping our identity to be more like his. So a proper understanding of our identity will be gained only as we relate to Jesus and grasp the fact that it is his image being formed in us. We do not look like him, yet we are growing to be like him in character as we get to know him more and more:

> *We are being transformed into the same image from one degree of glory to another. For this comes from the Lord who is the Spirit. (2 Corinthians 3:18)*

Since Jesus actually entered human existence we can be assured that being human must have mattered to him. His deep concern for us and his longing for us to belong to him are made clear in his willingness to go all the way to the cross.

> **We are growing to be like Jesus as we get to know him more and more**

(2) *We participate with Christ* from the moment we accept his free gift of salvation. By being linked to Christ we are linked to his heavenly Father. God is *our* Father, as Jesus declared to the crowd on the Galilee mountainside:

> *I am ascending to my Father and your Father. (Matthew 6:9; John 20:17)*

This connection we have with the Father is extraordinary. We are already being called *"children of God"* (1 John 3:1).

This is further illustrated by Paul in his statement that we are "made alive with Christ" (Ephesians 2:5). So an essential part of our identity is rooted in the fact that even while we are still in our human body we are already in an eternal relationship with God. He created us *"in his image"*; he sent his son Jesus to forgive our rebelliousness through his work on the cross; and the Holy Spirit came into our lives to transform us. Participating with Christ means that our identity has a dynamic dimension, because we are living with Jesus now and forever.

> *If anyone is in Christ, he is a new creation; the old has passed away, behold, the new has come. (2 Corinthians 5:17)*

This is further illustrated by Jesus in his description of the vine:

> *"Abide in me and I in you. As the branch cannot bear fruit by itself unless it abides in the vine, neither can you unless you abide in me." (John 15:4)*

This illustration helps us to understand that we are in an on-going relationship with Jesus. We are pruned on the vine and we are being moulded by this relationship. We are not to share in the world's values, but to grow day by day in the Christ-like nature which he has given us.

(3) *The power which moulds us*: this Christ-like nature can be understood through reading and applying God's written word to our lives. So Paul declares to the Ephesian Church:

> *In him you also, when you heard the word of truth, the gospel of your salvation, and believed in him, were sealed with the promised Holy Spirit, who is the guarantee of our inheritance until we acquire possession of it to the praise of his glory. (Ephesians 1:13–14)*

The Holy Spirit needs to be at work in us enabling us to be changing and responding to God's instructions. It is also interesting to note Paul's promise that the presence of the Holy Spirit in us is the guarantee that we are being sanctified — that is, being transformed. Paul does not necessarily distinguish between the Holy Spirit and Jesus (see Romans 8:9–11 above). If the Holy Spirit is working in us, then Christ is at work in us and we are in him.

Aspects of this moulding are found in the Beatitudes (Matthew 5): humility, compassion, love of one's enemy, a forgiving spirit (Matthew 18:21–22) and loving fellow Christians (John 15:9–12). It might also include accepting suffering for Christ even to the point of death for Christ (Mark 8:34 and 10:38). Suffering and death are very real challenges for those who live in places where Christians are under attack.

Acquiring these attributes and becoming committed to God's commands (John15:10–12) are best understood when we realise that the moulding we are talking about is the process of being sanctified. We can see this in Paul's first letter to the Corinthians (1:2): *"to those sanctified in Christ Jesus, called to be saints together..."*. Sanctification is the work of the Holy Spirit in us (John 3:34). It is a life-long process. As we read the Scriptures we ask the

Holy Spirit to point out aspects of our lives which need to be remoulded (John 14:26; and 16:13). We are indeed slowly becoming more Christ-like, becoming "holy" in putting on the new creation.

Clearly while we are on this earth complete conformity with the image of Christ is not possible, but as Paul said to the Corinthians:

> *we all…beholding the glory of the Lord, are being transformed into the same image from one degree of glory to another. For this comes from the Lord who is the Spirit. (2 Corinthians 3:18)*

There is no doubt that Jesus expects us to be growing into his new creation for we are to be "mature" (complete). Our true destiny is to fully reflect the image of God, not just through the "substantial" and "functional" dimensions but also at the "relational" level. Matthew records this statement in terms of "being perfect" (5:48) and Luke as "being merciful" (6:36). We are not being asked to imitate Christ, but rather to allow the Holy Spirit to transform us or to reproduce in us Christ-like qualities. These ideas are a reflection of the character of Christ and indicate the need for each one of us to go on growing so that our nature becomes more and more Christ-like (see Revelation 3:19–20). We will not be perfect whilst we live on earth, but we look to the Holy Spirit to keep changing us and moulding our identity into conformity with Christ (see Romans 12:2: *"be transformed by the renewing of your mind"*).

Questions for reflection or discussion

→ What has contributed to the growth of your faith over the years?

→ Examine Romans 12:9-21 and list the changes which could come into your life. Which of these changes have impacted or could impact your identity?

Chapter 13

Being in Christ — Part II

The fact that Christ will work with us is evidence of God's abundant grace and his calling to us to be part of his kingdom.

So being *in Christ and Christ in us* means being in a living relationship with Jesus in the power of the Holy Spirit. This is expressed by Peter in a fresh way:

> *Grow in the grace and knowledge of our Lord and Saviour Jesus Christ. To him be the glory both now and to the day of eternity. Amen. (2 Peter 3:18)*

God's grace is abundant

To continue our discussion about developing our identity we can add these points:

(4) *Being in Christ and having Christ in us* is another way of stating that *God's grace is abundant in us.* "Grace" is multi-faceted (see chapter 3). It is God's gift to us and includes his many blessings. We use the word "grace" to refer to God's provision enabling us to be saved and having the Holy Spirit in us enabling us to grow in the Christian life (sanctification). However, another important underlying theme is that grace is evidence of the continuing presence of God in our lives. It carries the sense of continuity. We are justified by God's grace as a gift (Romans 3:24) and our justification is a permanent state — unless we decide to reject Christ and his work of salvation. We are not to accept God's grace in vain (2 Corinthians 6:1). His grace is freely

bestowed on us (Ephesians 1:6–7) so that

> *Christ may dwell in your hearts through faith — that you, being rooted and grounded in love, may have strength to comprehend with all the saints what is the breadth and length and height and depth, and to know the love of Christ that surpasses knowledge, that you may be filled with all the fullness of God.* (Ephesians 3:17–19)

So being *in Christ and Christ in us* is a permanent status demonstrated by his love and reconciliation. His presence is not only a statement, but it is also a fact since we know that our being is filled by the wonderful presence of the triune God.

(5) Being in Christ means *a complete change of status*. There are two further aspects to this new status.

(5a) Firstly, our status is no longer judged in a legal way because God now responds positively to the fact that we have accepted his grace. God's act of grace is first of all his forgiveness available to us in Christ's work on the cross. Christ's act of forgiveness means that we are regarded by God as being justified. Being justified means that all our sins have been forgiven, assuming we have asked Jesus to forgive us, and we have repented of our sins. Repentance does not mean any loss of our identity, but it means that through personal confrontation our identity has been refreshed. For this reason we are not judged under the law, which we would be if we were still accountable for our disobedience to God, since our sins have been forgiven. But we are judged under the cross in that we have accepted Christ's death on the cross as the means of our salvation. By accepting Christ's offer of salvation, we are redeemed since Jesus has paid for our rebelliousness and regards us as totally forgiven. This is God's grace towards us. When Paul wrote to the Galatians stating, *"I have been crucified with Christ. It is no longer I who live, but Christ who lives in me"* (Galatians 2:20), he was declaring that he was no longer under the law. The cross and Christ's offer of justification meant for Paul that he was now a new person, indeed a redeemed person. Our focus on Jesus as our Lord requires our obedience to his word. Like us, this did not mean to Paul that once we gain our new status we do not sin, but it does mean that our intention is to be obedient to Jesus and that we will continue to thank Jesus for forgiving our sin. We also give thanks for the presence of the Holy Spirit in us assuring us of our saved status.

Our self-esteem is now deeply influenced by our status in Christ and our growing Christ-like character. For this reason, Paul could say that our true identity is in the *"cross... by which the world has been crucified to me and I to the world"* (Galatians 6:14) and *"we have the mind of Christ"* (1 Corinthians 2:16). We may consider ourselves as being united with Christ by being a member of the local church. This is a valuable activity since the church is the assembly of those who belong to Jesus. However, our identity as a Christian is not simply belonging to a church, but being identified with the crucified Christ. It is still appropriate to belong to a church as indicated by the writer of Hebrews who states that we should not forsake meeting together and so encourage one another (Hebrews 10:25). Meeting with fellow Christians can help us in our understanding of God's truth by discussing issues with them. At the same time we note that in belonging to a local church we are part of what the NT calls the "body of Christ". As the community of God's people he equips us so that the body of Christ may be built up:

> *until we all reach unity in the faith and in the knowledge of the Son of God and become mature, attaining to the whole measure of the fullness of Christ... speaking the truth in love, we will in all things grow up into him who is the head, that is, Christ. (Ephesians 4:12–15 TNIV)*

No wonder we can have self-respect and awareness of who we are now. We are redeemed in Christ! Our self-esteem emerges out of all that God-in-Christ has done for us. We not only have God's image, but we are also redeemed and in partnership with God. We are called to participate with him, to allow the Holy Spirit to transform us and to see God's grace working in us. This is a permanent shift when we grasp our new status as a child of God. We are in Christ and he is in us! What a wonderful blessing this is.

> *No longer a foreigner, but a citizen of the kingdom of God.*

(5b) Secondly, by being in Christ and he in us we are no longer foreigners but citizens of the kingdom of God. This fact of being members of a kingdom was announced by Jesus, *"The time is fulfilled, and the kingdom of God is at hand, repent and believe in the gospel"* (Mark 1:15). Jesus' statement is a declaration that with his coming into the world, his kingdom has arrived! Jesus means by this that his redeeming activity is available to all who will turn to him in faith. We may wish that we could see the political advantage of his being king, but we will have to wait for that event which will occur when Jesus Christ comes again. However, in the meantime we are members of God's family and in this capacity we bear the evidence of God's kingdom through showing forth God's righteousness (see chapters 4 and 12) and our growing Christ-like behaviour.

> No longer a foreigner but a citizen

This growth is dependent on our willingness to allow Christ to begin transforming our lives. The way we live, the things we do, the language we use, the standards we uphold in our family and in our everyday lives are essential reflections of God at work in us.

Paul's statement that we *"are being built together into a dwelling place for God by his Spirit"* (Ephesians 2:22) is making clear that our identity is established by being a member of God's kingdom. Here is an amazing status. God the Holy Spirit lives in us. No matter what others say, we know where we stand before the Creator. We have a living hope in Christ, we enjoy his love, and we desire to share his love with others. We do this by announcing this kingdom, this message of grace to the world. This is the missionary responsibility which Christ gave to his disciples and to us as members of his kingdom. We can do this because we are clear about our faith and therefore our Christ-like values. We know who we are! We have clarified our identity! We know what our lives should reflect! We know how we should live and rejoice in the fact that:

> *He has delivered us from the domain of darkness and transferred us to the kingdom of his beloved Son, in whom we have redemption, the forgiveness of sins. (Colossians 1:13–14)*

Being in Christ means that we reflect the values of the kingdom, apply these values to the society in which we live and show these values in our relationships with others. We are members both of Jesus' kingdom and the community in which we live. As a member of Jesus' kingdom we should also make a stance in our community for our faith. In this way we can have some impact for the kingdom, its presence and its values. In these practical ways we will be giving evidence of our new identity status as members of the kingdom of God.

Questions for reflection or discussion

- → What rights and obligations can a person expect as a member of a kingdom on earth?
- → What rights and obligations can a person expect as a member of God's kingdom?

Chapter 14

What Makes Us What We Are Now?

We can grasp the fact of our own dignity, but we must also pursue human rights for others and establish the base for this in our own values.

One of my responsibilities during the 1990s was as President of the United Mission to Nepal. This mission agency engaged some 340 experts from around the world and we trained over 4000 Nepalis in a wide range of skills. Our agency was very concerned for the Nepalis living in the mountains as they suffered various indignities. They had little medical or educational assistance and many had to walk up and down mountains each day to get water and sticks for their cooking fires. We also had many refugees from Tibet who needed housing and food. As we sought to find the most effective way to develop long-term assistance for the Nepalis and the Tibetans, we had to give careful thought to three questions: how to help the local people find their own *dignity*, how to promote *human rights* and what *values* did we want to promote. These questions became integral to what we tried to do to help the local people develop skills. Reflecting on these questions can also strengthen us in our understanding of our own personal identity.

> We are inheritors of an eternal future with Jesus, this is his gift to us and we can claim this from him

Our own dignity

Earlier chapters in this book have outlined that we are made in the image of God. This means that we have a moral capacity, a rational strength, and an ability to distinguish ourselves from everyone else. Another aspect of the image of God in us is that we have emotions which enable us to develop our desires and which will influence our attitudes. One of the most significant aspects of being created by God is the freedom we have inherited from him as part of his image in us. This freedom is a sign of the dignity we have as a human person, regardless of what view we might have of the divine. Along with these personal factors we have our memories and past experiences, all or some of which will impact the present development of these factors in us. Through these memories, experiences and our moral and rational capacities we will determine what are our own values and these values will clarify who we are in our own eyes and in the eyes of others.

> Freedom is a sign of the dignity which everyone has, but it needs to be promoted

Our identity is enhanced by grasping whatever freedoms are available to us and this includes our rights as citizens and as human beings. Freedom allows us to pursue our own thoughts, ideas, faith and relationships, and thus with freedom we can pursue and strengthen our self-image. In contrast, subservience reduces our self-image and self-confidence.

Because we are created with dignity which we inherited from our Creator, we do matter not only to God, but also to ourselves and we should matter to others. When we are treated as someone who does not matter, our identity suffers enormously. I could see that a Nepali living in the city of Kathmandu, where most of the facilities were available, could regard the very poor people living in the mountains as being of little worth. After all these people didn't "contribute to Nepal as a nation in any way". One of the political groups saw them as worthless. Our role in the agency was to promote their value. In such circumstances we needed to remind ourselves that regardless of how the mountain people were being treated they mattered to God and so they mattered to us. This is not only valid, but a necessary part of the right to be human and to exist. At the same time we recognise that having rights means that we also have responsibilities. By way of example, we have a responsibility to be obedient to the national law and to those the nation has appointed to be in authority. Yet this responsibility is measured against the right one has for fair treatment.

At the same time we should be aware that our own view of our dignity can mislead us. We are not necessarily morally good! We have dignity as a person because we have inherited this from our Creator. Only for this reason we can say that dignity is an essential part of who we are. But we then add to this inherited dignity further valuation of ourselves which will reflect the sort of person we are and how we act in various situations. If our sense of importance leads us to being proud of ourselves then we may have crossed the subtle boundary of sinfulness. As Paul said to the Romans:

> *Do not think of yourself more highly than you ought, but rather think of yourself with sober judgment, in accordance with the measure of faith God has given to you. (Romans 12:3)*

How this becomes real in our own lives is influenced by the fact that *"your life is now hidden with Christ in God"* (Colossians 3:3), and see chapter 8 above.

Human rights and justice

The Universal Declaration of Human Rights (1948) affirms our rights, dignity and worth. However, some countries are not obedient to this declaration and Muslim countries are subject to the "Cairo Declaration on Human Rights in

> Human rights and justice need to be promoted, personally and nationally

Islam" (1990) which subjects all people to Sharia legal requirements.[21] Non-Muslims in Islamic countries are also subject to Sharia and also to the requirements of the *dhimmi* [22] concept. This concept degrades and dehumanises non-Muslims in a range of ways. All this means is that while we have inalienable rights, these rights need to be established and promoted. We need to both identify our own rights and also clearly establish in our own lives and the way we function what we consider to be the rights of others. Rights do not just happen, they need to be achieved and so in every organisation with which we are involved we should promote the need for dignity and the rights of all. Rights are not automatic, they need to be established in the life of the community and so not be ignored.

As we consider the rights which should be applied both by ourselves individually and by our nation we automatically think about issues of *justice*. There is a strong theme in the Scriptures on "justice" and this word is linked to the word "righteousness". These terms are a statement about the nature of God. He is the righteous one and he expects us to reflect his character by seeking justice and pursuing righteousness. This is explained in biblical passages such as this one: *"let justice roll down like waters, and righteousness an ever-flowing stream"* Amos 5:24. (See also Psalm 103:6; Isaiah 5:7; Jeremiah 22:3–4; Micah6:8; and Romans 3:21–22.)

The questions I asked the team in Nepal are questions we need to ask ourselves. Does our identity reflect justice and do our actions demonstrate a commitment to righteousness? Whatever we demonstrate does tell others something about who we are. This is our identity!

---

21 Sharia requirements are found in the Qur'an and the associated books written by Muhammad's followers known as the Hadiths.
22 The *dhimmi* concept in Islam is the way Muslims treat and "protect" non-Muslims in some societies such that non-Muslims are second-class citizens and are humiliated by the Muslim community. For detail see Mark Durie, *The Third Choice*, (Melbourne: Deror Books, 2010) and David Claydon (ed) *Islam, Human Rights and Public Policy*, (Melbourne: Acorn Press, 2009).

Our values

Our dignity and human worth can also be a reflection of the values which we hold. We determine and/or assume our personal values from our upbringing, our world view (which includes our religious and/or philosophical base), our personal experiences, our emotions, and our community. We work out our values as we interact with the different dimensions of society and as we determine what sort of person we want to be. These values are the rules and evaluations we apply to ourselves and they cover all aspects of our own life and involvements. Values also enable us to determine how we think others should function in the various situations in which we find ourselves. Our own values and what we think the values of others are, or should be, are major factors in declaring our own identity. In some situations we may function according to our values. In other situations we may not have yet worked out our values-base and so we tend to make a decision on what we think will produce the most convenient outcome.

> Our values determine our identity and our current friendships can determine our values!

Adolescents may tend to be pragmatic responding to the expectations of their friends. In this way others may see some teenagers functioning in unsatisfactory ways, but as the teenagers continue to grow they may develop a mature set of personal values. Parental input and religious grounding can be very formative in this process. Rational self-regulation may become evident in this assembling of values. The development of personal values can mean that we develop our personal stature. When this happens our identity becomes established in our own eyes and in the eyes of others and this gives us both a sense of confidence in who we are and freedom to be the person we want to be.

The NT uses a number of words which indicate God's purpose for us. These are summed up by Peter:

> *You also, like living stones, are being built into a spiritual house to be a holy priesthood, offering spiritual sacrifices acceptable to God through Jesus Christ... you are a chosen people, a royal priesthood, a holy nation, a people belonging to God that you may declare the praises of him who called you out of darkness into his wonderful light. Once you were not a people of God, but now you are a people of God; once you had not received mercy, but now you have received mercy. (1 Peter 2:4,5,9,10)*

This passage really does sum up who I am and who you are.

Living stones: You are part of the household of faith and, together with the other Christians, are being built into Christ's church on earth. Jesus is the living stone and he is the head of the church and we are living stones making up the church. We are being built up together. We should work together to help one another grow and so be built up as his people in this his world.

A chosen people: God has called us to be his children, to belong to his family and forever to be in his kingdom.

A royal priesthood: This refers to the personal sacrifice of praise we offer to Jesus the King. Our prime focus is to bring to God our praise because he is our King and we are given the title of being royals for we are members of his family and we thank him for what he has done for us.

A holy nation, a people belonging to God: This picks up the OT identification of the children of Israel as God's people and thus they were a holy nation. We are his precious treasure, the object of his affection. All those who belong to God are today's holy nation. So our identity is rooted in being part of God's nation and this supersedes membership in our earthly nation. This doesn't mean that we ignore our earthly connections, status and responsibilities, but that these connections are subservient to being a member of God's kingdom.

People who declare the praises of him who called us: This now dominates our life and our identity in all that we do.

People who have received mercy: The saving work of Jesus Christ enables us to be justified and frees us to be part of his kingdom.

Questions for reflection or discussion

→ What do you consider are some of the basic human rights a person should expect from society?

→ What can/ should a person do when these rights are not provided or are deliberately ignored or removed?

Chapter 15

The Emerging Identity through the Growing Years

We change as we develop our sense of self and our capacity to respond to various situations — this can impact our choice of friends.

Stages of Development

Young people have many challenges to relate to. They need to know who they are in terms of the static features (ethnicity, gender, nationality) of their existence. They also need to determine at various stages of their lives their own personal features, their own self-image, and the self-esteem they can gain from within the social groups and institutions to which they belong. There will be change throughout the adolescent life and indeed throughout most of their lives.

Here is an outline of stages in identity development:

Conformity — Young children usually accept without question or discussion the values of their parents and the culture in which they live. In many traditional societies this period of conformity continues through puberty and into adulthood.

Dissonance — In early adolescence young people become aware of different values and ways of behaving, and develop some capacity to make choices.

Resistance — Adolescents begin to be influenced by these "different voices" and may question for reflection or discussion the standards of their parents. They experiment with different identities modelled on the images they receive through the media, role models and family. They may have multiple identities, changing them to fit in with the group they are with. They will seek to see themselves as an individual with personal rights and not as an appendage to their parents, and thus not necessarily need to be obedient to parents. This can become a time of conflict, requiring love and patience by the adolescent as well as parents and teachers.

Immersion — In this stage young people can become totally absorbed by their peers and other role models. This is a dangerous stage. If they are overwhelmed by the group and lose their own individuality, they can become like puppets in the hands of others. One sees this particularly in gangs and at "party" events.

Introspection — They begin to question through reflection or discussion the voices which influence them and start to make decisions for themselves about how they will live. They begin to form their own unique identity.

Synergy — They select the best (or what they want!) from all the role models around them, including their parents, and arrive at their own personally satisfying set of values and behaviours, achieving a sense of identity and wellbeing.[23]

As adolescents move through these stages there can be ambiguity in their identity. Some aspects of youthful identity will show on the outside of the person, such as in music, clothing and tattooing. But none of these elements necessarily indicates the personal identity of the adolescent. All it

---

23   Used by permission from Howard Groome. This appeared in Scripture Union International *Catalyst*, August 2008, Issue 4, p6; with a few additions by this author.

reveals is a stage at which the person is rebelling, or discovering, or relating to a group with whom she or he wishes to belong. Thus public behaviour may be artificial and the real person submerged for a time.

Affirmation and trust

There are some major factors in adolescents as they come to terms with themselves and clarify for themselves who they are. These will usually be:

- Affirmation from family members and from some of the members of whatever group they belong to;
- Results of sporting and/or academic activities;
- Features of personal imagination — working out what one could be, or could do, or how to respond to a significant person who has mistreated or treated them well;
- The static characteristics (ethnicity and gender) and how others respond to these;
- The false images one wants to give of one's self; and
- The style or level of independence which one has or could have.

As a young person becomes an adult, there is usually some attempt at determining one's values and world-view and some reflection on one's emotions and how these could be controlled. Thus the person is starting to determine the basic identity as to who he or she is. As the young adult moves into a work position, the role may have some influence on the identity, but more likely the friendships developed in this new group setting will have their impact on personal self-worth even though the young adult is not usually aware of the developing personal identity.

Some young people become members of local or street gangs. Such groups have definite requirements for membership both to enter and to belong to. In other words, there is an authority structure in place and this structure can be very demanding and will overwhelm the individual adolescent. When I spent some time with some gang members in Chicago I found that in certain streets a male adolescent could not survive if he did not belong to the street gang. Entry to the gang was gained by killing another person and continuing membership meant involvement in fighting other street gangs. Submission to the authority of the self-appointed leaders of a gang was responded to by the young men as a way to survive. The only way out was by moving to a different district. Those I talked to had a vague Christian background and were hoping to become leaders of their opposing gangs. They imagined that they could change the goals of their gangs and develop helpful values among these other young people. I didn't stay there long enough to see if they could grasp the authority they needed to become leaders and if then they could bring about such a change. However, it did highlight for me the influence of some in the neighbourhood who may bring pressure on others to be helpful and pursue positive goals as against those who are already in leadership and pressure others to change their values and accept committing crimes as an exercise of personal survival.

> Authority structures can be overwhelming

It was interesting for me in such a setting to note that the norms or expectations of these gang members had been adjusted to suit the street requirements, but that their values of what is good and right had not changed. I guess that this was a cause for confusion which showed up in the home and in school. One of the areas of confusion can be in the level of trust. Who is trusting whom and under what circumstances? Trust is the "cement" which holds people together. The absence of trust can result in unhealthy independence and an independent adolescent usually finds it difficult to communicate with others. Trust can also be the bridge between self-understanding as an interdependent person (that is a person who is communicating with others) and what the person does with his/her own life. However, trust is not the only factor at work in a person's life. There are many other elements as indicated above, such as authority, friendships and affirmative or negative comments, which are not necessarily consistent yet are part of everyone's life. So it is helpful to be aware that there can be a fragmentation of factors which make up the self. Adults need to find ways of enabling adolescents to work their way through the concept of authority and trust or any area of confusion with a view to maintaining a connection with the adolescent in the longer term. Church youth groups can assist in this by developing programs in which trust is a feature and through which trust in Jesus can be recognised.

> Emotional or physical child abuse has a long-term dramatic impact on the whole of a person's life

Cyber identity and a growing self-concept

The pattern for many adolescents is to use social networking as a way to display identity. Cyberspace provides an interesting forum for people to appear not to communicate with anyone in particular, and yet still also make oneself known to a closed circle of friends. The impact of this method of connecting with others is to actually minimise most of one's attributes, because others will only know what is written on facebook or twitter. At the same time it may mean that what is written is a significant aspect of an adolescent's self-concept. Unfortunately, what others write about the recipient may be abusive and have a drastic emotional impact on this person. One's identity can suffer as the recipient reads nasty comments. Help is often needed as one seeks to ignore or to absorb what someone else says. Our identity should not be moulded by negative comments of others. At this stage of life, young people usually start to determine for themselves who they are. This growing self-concept develops as a culmination of all the experiences, friendships and authority events which the adolescent has had. Affirmations and criticisms made by those we know and respect, as well as rewards, hopes and conflicts together with all the experiences remembered will enable the person to determine who she or he is. Personal identity thus can become clearer.

As adolescents move towards adulthood they will develop this self-concept. Unfortunately for some there are very sad events in the past. Child abuse, whether physical or emotional, usually features strongly in adult memory, and it affects behaviour and psychological balance. When the person is aware of this, then identity can become greatly affected. While some will repress the traumatic memories of early years, yet in late adolescence or adulthood they may start to remember some of the detail and struggle with this as they try to determine what actually happened. Unpredictable or frightening family or school environments may also cause an adolescent to "disconnect" from these past times of stress. This dissociation from the past helps them to "box" these memories "away", but the impact of the trauma remains with them.

Every child notes the environment and the people nearby as the child grows. All these facts are stored in the memory forever even though the memory may not bring some of the information to the fore until one is much older. Each encounter of the child's body and mind will affect personality development in later adolescence or in adulthood. Every child and adolescent deserves to be free to grow up in a safe and stable environment so that their personal self-esteem is matched by their growing body and brain.

Every adult should be aware of the enormous and permanent damage they can do to the person not only when that person is a child, but throughout the rest of his or her life. All those who have been abused need to know how important they are before God and how professional assistance may help.

Bullying will also impact the life both of the bullied person and the bully, and this can result in these people performing in unsatisfactory ways with life-long consequences. Adolescence is a fragile period of life and young people do need to be protected from serious negative experiences even if they themselves do not always realise their need of this. Bullying by peers or adults is damaging. Gang-like authority is also very damaging. Young people need to be warned of these negative possibilities at an early stage of their lives by their parents and teachers so that the level of trust in parents and teachers is enhanced by the honest comments of adults close to them.

Self-concept is a complex aspect of a person's life. The adolescent brings together into some equilibrium all the experiences, affirmations and criticisms in such a way that personal understanding emerges. This self-concept is then tested against new challenges and tasks. If these attempts at proof fail then the process either starts over again or suffers from massive disruption and confusion. Working this out can be a lonely task and many adolescents require time to think about some of these issues. Others may simply function without much thought as long as their hopes are achieved. Some may try to function as an "ideal-self" which means pretending to function as a different person perhaps like someone they have seen in the movies or on the sports field. By failing to discover their own self-concept they will find it difficult to determine who they really are and how they should function. Christian youth groups can help their members to think about these personal issues and outline the need to see themselves as "being in Christ".

Questions for reflection or discussion

→ What are some of the issues young people have to face in adolescent years?

→ What are some of the issues adults may have to face as a result of childhood or adolescent experiences?

→ What are some useful guidelines for an adult to respond to in a workplace, or committee, or in local church situation, if being bullied?

Chapter 16

My Humility and Identity

We are God's workmanship, created in Christ Jesus to do good works. (Ephesians 2:8–10)

The biblical position

Humility is regarded as a fundamental dimension of personal identity. Yet this raises the issue as to whether I can promote who I am in a situation where I should make myself better known and at the same time be humble.

We have inherited from our birth parents our ethnicity and our gender (our "static" features) which identify us to others in a superficial way. But most of us are keen to demonstrate other aspects of who we really are. In my work in Nepal I found that I needed to encourage Nepalis to undertake a particular task and learn how to pursue that task so that they could be helped to discover their abilities. Discovering something they could do well contributed to a more positive self-image. I also had an opportunity to share with them about my Christian faith and how my self-image developed by realising that God has given us gifts. These gifts need to be expressed and the exciting outworking of these gifts is shown in three ways:

a. our "love" for others, in other words our concern for others and their needs, as well as our love of Jesus as our Lord and Saviour;

b. our "hope" in the certainty of who Jesus is and his involvement in our lives; and

      c.   our "faith" in Jesus, for he is the one in whom we commit ourselves.

These gifts are recorded in 1 Corinthians 12:31. These are God's gift to us. We don't have to be someone special to demonstrate these aspects of our identity. This outline of what is available to all generated discussion among my Nepali friends about abilities and gifts and why Jesus is part of this expression of gifts. I explained that for Christians there are some guidelines and expectations.

Firstly, self-esteem is not a statement of pride, it is an honest acceptance of our own gifts and potentials, as well as the fact of God's presence and gifts in us. We thank God for whatever we are able to do.

Secondly, the biggest gift we have is that we have inherited an eternal future which is a result of our present relationship with Jesus. We are entirely dependent on Jesus and his gracious gift of salvation and membership in his family. We haven't worked for this status, but we praise the Lord for it.

Later, among those Nepalis who had already become Christians I went on to add:

Thirdly, the spiritual gifts we have are given to us by the Holy Spirit. We do not see ourselves as important just because we have the gift of prayer, of healing or of speaking, but we thank Jesus for whatever gifts we have (Romans 12:3–8; 1 Corinthians 1:7–12; 1 Peter 4:10–11). On some occasions we seem to be enabled by the Holy Spirit to exercise a particular gift with good results and yet we may not be able to exercise this gift again. This is also the Holy Spirit's decision and we accept it as his work. On other occasions we may be using our various gifts to assist others, but these are also gifts from our Creator and *"we are God's workmanship, created in Christ Jesus to do good works"* (Ephesians 2:8–10).

Fourthly, there is a spirit of humility which we are asked to exercise according to the Beatitudes. These challenge us to be *"meek"* (i.e. gentle, lacking pretension), *"merciful"* and *"peacemakers"* (Matthew 5). This does not mean ignoring our abilities. Rather it means to recognise our strengths, be self-critical about our weaknesses, and affirm the abilities of others.

Fifthly, our response to the call by Jesus is to deny ourselves and take up our cross and follow him (Matthew 16:24–28). The emphasis is on self-denial, on a committment to being "in Christ" and on the willingness to suffer for Jesus. This is clearly a position of humility, even to the point of suffering. Dietrich Bonhoeffer explained this by the words: "When Christ calls a man [sic], he bids him come and die".[24]

Sixthly, we are referred to by Jesus as being part of "the vine". He is the main part of this vine and if we are connected to him, then we are the branches and as branches we are to show life and fruit (= making the gospel known) otherwise we are of no use (John 15:1–8). Our identity is made clear by the fact that we are connected to Jesus and we are to demonstrate this aspect of our identity by making known the gospel (the fruit of the vine).

Some general guidelines

1. What sort of personality do we want to project? There usually are some situations where we need to make known our capabilities and experience so as to gain, for instance, a job or a scholarship. This is specific and valid. The way we present the details will usually be in accordance with the requirements of the organisation. Normally, we would state the facts without overstating our achievements. In some settings it is appropriate to have a person recommend us and this person can be stronger than we would be in the presentation.

2. We may be a speaker at an event and the MC will introduce us. In some countries this introduction has to be extensive so that those in attendance know more about us. In most countries this need not be extensive, in which case we can indicate to the MC what to say which is relevant to the audience. When we do speak about our abilities and

---

24 *The Cost of Discipleship*, London: SCM, 1937, p7.

experience this will often show through in our actions or words, so that there is normally no need to say very much beyond those features which may not be obvious.

3. Personal promotion is best made through what we do and what we say, rather than by giving a description of our gift(s) or of the wonderful results we have had from exercising our gift(s).

4. There are some in our community who are powerful. They may have valid reasons for their power or they may be bullies (one biblical example is Goliath's threat to the Israelites in 1 Samuel 17). While in many cases we have to accept the role of the powerful, there are times when we can object. In the case of government bureaucracies there may be a government commission to which we can complain, or we may have to challenge our local Member of Parliament about the issue. Another way is to report the situation to the media. In all these situations we are also acting powerfully. The fact is that individuals often do have some element of power even though this is pursued with personal humility. In some countries there is no official way of dealing with bureaucratic power and bribes are sometimes used, but as a Christian we seek not to use bribes as a weapon.

5. Speaking out can be a means of responding to an antagonistic act. We can choose to do so if justice is being sought. Silence allows the offender to re-offend. Often ordinary people in the community are able to bring an offensive behaviour to an end by speaking out to the media and sometimes by doing something which catches the attention of others, such as a long-distance walk supported financially for the cause. Acting in this way allows our identity to be a stance for justice which often is recognised.

6. We may look out for others in our midst who may be shy and not readily finding friends. Inviting such a person into our school group or our home Bible study or some other activity can be enormously encouraging for this person.

7. Taking a lead may be the way forward in some situations. Quite often there is a leadership vacuum. No-one takes the lead. Or a person takes some of the lead and by failing to fully take the lead some wrong things occur. We can fill the gap by showing leadership through acting in an appropriate way. By doing so others will see that we have some leadership ability. In taking such action we may still be humble in the way we do this, but we are also revealing an aspect of our identity.

History has shown how women and men have sometimes filled a gap and by stepping into it, they enable good things to happen. Stepping into a small gap as against taking on the whole role, may well mean that we are acting humbly. Of course it may be that others want us to fill the whole role at some point of time. And there is no problem in doing that, particularly when others want us to do so. For instance, Florence Nightingale (1820–1910) demonstrated how the wounded could be cared for. As a result of her acts of mercy others later took the full leadership role of medical care for the wounded and the Red Cross was founded. Rosa Parks (1913–85) decided not to give her seat in the bus to a white man and this act of defiance against being bullied resulted in the civil rights reform. She did only one small thing, but others then took the full leadership of the "rights" movement. Her act was certainly one of humility.

> Undertaking a small role can highlight the need for stronger action which others may take up

8. Some of the points above touch also on justice. We have a right to ask for human rights for ourselves and others. The Scriptures expect us to require justice and to care for the poor, the widow and the orphan (i.e. the vulnerable people; Jeremiah 4:11; Amos 5:24; Micah 6:8). We will need to be an advocate for the right and we may need to be assertive, but by being assertive we need to be willing to be criticised and to engage with the critics. This is different from being aggressive which

means being demanding and unwilling to debate. We can be assertive while not losing our personal humility and dignity.

9. In most situations where we need to argue for a cause we need to work out a strategy. For this it can be helpful to talk the matter through with others and perhaps have their assistance as we pursue the issue. Perhaps our willingness to engage others in the process of thinking and acting is further evidence of our personal humility. It also expresses our identity as a person since we want to be in a relationship and want to engage with others. It is useful to have this in mind since we are not self-sufficient!

Questions for reflection or discussion

→ Look up 1 Samuel 17 and note the ways in which Goliath "bullied" David. How did David prevail?

→ Are acts of civil disobedience justified?

Chapter 17

National and Community Identities

Our speech and our clothes can become indicators of our identity. Symbols are used as a way of indicating particular identities.

The identity attached to us may be misleading

We understand ourselves in part as a consequence of how others see us. The way others recognise us is in itself influenced by the community or tribe to which we belong. This is particularly obvious if we belong to a minority group which exists in a wider community. It is also obvious if we grew up in another country and reflect the speech rhythm of that country, or wear the clothes of that country or of the religious community to which we belong — we would then be identified as belonging to another community. When my wife and I were in Pakistan, Robyn chose to wear a "shalwar kameez" so as to identify with the local women among whom she was ministering. Some of the women took her down to the bazaar and helped her buy culturally appropriate dress. She chose the most colourful she could find!

There are consequences to being identified as being different from the local community. The identity attached to us may be totally unreasonable and in fact misleading, or it may accurately describe an aspect of our values and intentions. Identification through this means may not fairly determine our personalities or how we see ourselves. Yet there will be some aspects which are likely to be correct.

Multi-cultural identity

Multiculturalism contributes to distinguishing communities and identifying members of each local community and this can cause the segregation of these communities and even conflict between them. Community tensions of every type can generate antagonisms and cause some members to flaunt their religious or cultural features. In promoting obvious features, there is a tendency to focus not on the cultural dimensions but on the religious aspect of clothing and public activities. One can see this among some of the religious minorities in our midst. This can bring discredit to a religious group or cause the wider community to focus on the faults of the religion when a person dresses or acts in a way which is regarded as unacceptable to others. Examples of this can be seen after terrorist events in various countries and one result is that people wearing clothes which reveal that they have the same religion as the terrorists get blamed for the terrorist's actions. They are lumped together on religious grounds and their real identities are not considered.

Another consequence of this is that some people may choose to wear the clothing of a particular religious group and so further promote their religious community identity. In this way they fail to develop themselves in a way which would enable them to be more acceptable in the country where they are living. It is by adapting to the dress code of the nation where they live that enables others to look beyond the clothing and start to discover the real identity of these people. The fact is that our real identity is not just automatic. We have to create and sustain who we are by the way we function and relate to others. The way we are recognised does impact the understanding we have of ourselves and our identity.

> Our real identity is not automatic

Symbols proclaiming identity

Most religions, clubs and commercial operations have an identity promoted through symbols and through buildings of a particular style. This style may indicate the religious connection of the building. These symbols are usually regarded as special and not to be copied by others. They indicate the identity of the company and of the religion. Symbols highlight the social or commercial identity of the members while allowing each person to maintain his or her own individual identity. Attachment to a symbol by any individual, such as a cross or a Star of David on a necklace, may indicate to others this person's religious connections. Others make decisions on the basis of the symbols they see. School children in many countries wear uniforms unique to their school and these identify the school to which each belongs without minimising each one's own identity, but making known to the community the social identity of the institution.

Cultural identity in the community

In the case of Christians in a non-Christian nation, there is the need to work out in what ways they can dress and act according to the local culture, yet hold to the values and the doctrine which emanate from the Scriptures. For the Christian, personal identity is rooted in Jesus Christ and not in clothing or other cultural activities. All our experiences, ideas and hopes can be set aside if we need to because our ultimate identity is "being in Jesus". This position is very clear in the life of Dietrich Bonhoeffer who, in his prison poem "Who am I?", ended with these words:

> *Whoever I am, Thou knowest, O God, I am Thine!* [25]

In relating to other cultures and to people of other religions, it can be helpful to be aware of the position taken in respect to both community and personal identity. This can help us to look beyond the religious dimension and seek to recognise the personal identity of each person.

---

25 Eberhard Bethge, *Dietrich Bonhoeffer: Letters and Papers from Prison*, (London: SCM Press 1953), p.165.

Other aspects of national identity

Many nations promote their own national patriotism through symbols such as flags and anthems, and often through sporting successes. The nation may identify itself through its history and culture and may produce promotional films to gain tourists. If a nation sees itself as being criticised by other nations, there are usually attempts at reacting to this. One way is to strengthen the attitude of the citizens by promoting what a great nation/people they are. This in itself enlarges the people's self-identity as they become more patriotic. Another mechanism used is to strengthen the nation's defence systems to prove to the world how important they are. This may have only a small impact on the identity of the citizens. Yet another way forward is to develop products which people in other countries want. Citizens in some countries have difficulty determining what is their national identity, although this often becomes more apparent to those who travel out of the country for a period of time. Winning in international sporting events can enlarge the awareness of national identity and this can give an element of pride to the individual and thus have some impact on a person's self-awareness.

There is one other challenge which some nations have faced since the 1950s and that is the decline of the world view/philosophy of the nation. For instance, Italy dropped its fascist position after WWII and the people turned more strongly to the Catholic tradition and to a political world view of democracy. Likewise when Communism collapsed in the 1990s in Eastern Europe the leaders of the mass opposition movement were already committed to their Christian faith and this faith filled much of the world-view vacuum and it became an essential part of their personal identities. However, when this happened in the USSR there was a notable lack of anything to replace Communism. Religion has become strong in the lives of some, particularly in the Central Asian Republics, but there are many in Russia who today still feel lost finding an empty space in their identity which has not been filled by another world view. Ultimately, individuals need a political scheme as part of their collective identity and nations need to survive as nations. Whatever way this is pursued it is likely to impact personal identities.

Questions for reflection or discussion

→ What symbols identify your nation?

→ Reflect on the Christian symbols which you or others might wear. Have they sometimes proved to be a talking point?

Chapter 18

Identities Determined by Religion

Religious affiliation can strengthen one's identity. Yet religious doctrine and dogmas usually impact the way one thinks and behaves.

Self-image is to some extent a product of religious or philosophical requirements

Community and national identities are often formed by religious affiliation and/or by a commitment to an ideology.[26] Both religion and ideology give rise to a system of thought about what is true and not true, and an attitude towards the world. Some countries will not allow citizens to change their religious identity and where this occurs the government ensures that everyone has an identity card. A legal system which resists apostasy (that is rejection) from the national religion means that there is no genuine freedom of religion or speech, and this lack of freedom creates divisions in the community. It also means that personal identities may be hidden or that minorities have tough challenges in pursing a personal identity of their choice.

A religious dimension to one's identity can assist in establishing bonds between the members of a religion and this can give a sense of stability

---

26 An ideology or what can be called a "world view" is a system of thought and emotion about the world, society and other people, and both personal and national decisions emerge from this ideological position.

> Both nations and organisations such as schools and sporting clubs like to have a self-image of achievement and this can strengthen the identity of individuals

particularly for minority groups. Through this mechanism members can strengthen their personal identity with the religious commitment required by the larger group. Whilst this is usually helpful in minority religious communities, it can lead to nominalism among some of those belonging to large religious groups.

Some people find themselves committed to a world view or a philosophy of life which for them determines how they see the world, the people in the world and other nations. Such a philosophy can strengthen one's self-image as one aligns oneself to the philosophical declarations about others and thus about oneself.

For Christians our identity is principally determined by the fact that we know we are created by God and so we desire to reflect his values, his identity of love and of partnership with him, and thus seeking to live "in Christ". Our values, experiences, ideas and the way others recognise us also have a significant impact as we evaluate our own identity. Those who follow other religions have their identities moulded by the teaching of those religions.

My early life in different settings was such that I learnt something about the Islamic and the Hindu religions. Then during the 14 years I served with the Church Missionary Society I spent time not only with missionaries but also with local people in some 50 countries. This enabled me to talk to people about their religious ideas and to find out what are some of the more hidden driving forces in their religion. It is out of these discussions that I can write about the identities of people in each faith.

Hindu self-image

For Hindus, their self-image is influenced by two major factors. The first is the person's caste — this status determines a person's position in society and having this status helps influence the way one views oneself and determines how one can relate to others in the community. The other factor is that everyone is divine. There is one "god" who is supreme, namely, Brahman. While divinity may be seen in one or more of the estimated 330 million "gods", nevertheless this Brahman is the principle of life. Hindus believe it inhabits every part of existence. It is impersonal and unknowable. So the spiritual goal of a Hindu is to become one with Brahman, and thus cease to exist as an "individual self" (known as *moksha*). In this way one can be released from the deeds or sins of previous existences (*karma*). Until *moksha* is achieved, Hindus believe that they will be repeatedly reincarnated in order that they may work towards self-realisation of the truth (the truth being that only Brahman exists, nothing else). For this reason one should not intervene in a person's poverty, because by doing so one interrupts the cosmic process of reincarnation. So personal identity has no particular value in itself, but one slowly gains value as one recognises the continuity of reincarnation and the slow reform of the individual. Through the reincarnation process one's failings can be paid off (through the sufferings in each incarnation of life) as one gets close to Brahman, but there is no earthly, religiously connected idea of personal identity.

It is interesting to note that the lowest caste in Hindu society is the Dalits — the untouchables. A write-up about them[27] indicates that these people have no dignity and no self-worth; they are not even allowed to enter the inner sanctums of Hindu temples. Those Dalits who have been converted to faith in Jesus have then realised that they are dignified people and they have found their identity in Jesus. This new realisation of their true identity is supported by church fellowship, the sacraments, adherence to Scripture and devotion to Christ.

---

27 Samuel Jayakumar, *Dalit Consciousness and Christian Conversion*, (Dehli: ISPCK, 1999) p. 224.

Buddhist self-image

Self-identity is found as one recognises that passion and personal desires are the cause of suffering, and only as one sets aside those passions can one develop a sense of self. However, within strict Buddhism there is no permanent self or soul.[28] So people see themselves as existing because they are following the "Eightfold Path" which includes right beliefs, feelings, speech, conduct, effort and memory.[29] One's identity exists only while walking this earth and is found by being committed to the Eightfold Path of rightness. It is then by being obedient to Guatama's[30] commandments that one achieves Nirvana where there is no self and so the cycle of rebirth has come to an end. This emphasis on one's personal thoughts and the setting aside of passions creates a strong sense of moral behaviour and the vacuum can be filled with a willingness to love all other people and animals.

Behind this lies the view that there is no difference between physical and spiritual realities and thus no distinction between humans, animals and objects. Hence, personal identity and self-worth are not an issue and are not discussed, since no matter what the differences are between people and things it does not matter since all people and animals will experience ultimately Nirvana. The moral code does involve respect for Buddhist monks, but this is because of their status in the Buddhist hierarchy. The Christian can use the Eightfold Path in conversation as a means of opening up the difference between personal achievement and allowing God to be the one who totally saves and changes the person. The fact that the person also matters to the Creator is a concept that can take time to convey. What a difference to know that we matter to our Creator for ever!

---

28   Peter Santina in http://www.buddhanet.net/funbud13.htm cited 13/5/11. "No self" is known as anatma.
29   For detail see David Claydon, *Connecting Across Cultures*, (Brunswick East: Acorn Press, 2nd edn. 2000), p.102.
30   The founder of Buddhism.

Muslim self-image

The fundamental basis for identity as a Muslim is rooted in the *Shahada* (creed), the *Sharia* (law), and the *ummah* (collective identity, the community). As Abd al-Wahab el-Effendi[31] noted, the difference between national identity and a Muslim's personal identity is that the Muslim is accountable to Allah in all things[32] and to the collective community of all Muslim people.

Thus, a Muslim will hold strongly to the creed and regard this as the foremost expression of one's world view. This fixed expression of the creed (fixed in word content and meaning) is the starting point leading to a less personal identity. The individual has no capacity to express her or his relationship with Allah in the way she or he may desire or think appropriate and helpful. One sees this expressed in the longing when many Muslims say they would love to get closer to Allah. Or, in contrast, one sees this in Najib Mahfuz's statement that "God does not relate to me and I cannot relate to him. There is nothing but dead silence between us."[33] This can be further understood by the fact that whilst the Qur'an declares Allah to be the Creator, there is no statement about human beings being created in Allah's image (Qur'an 2:29). See chapter 2 about the Christian understanding and the impact of being created in God's image, and that we matter to God and therefore to each other. What Muslims do believe is that they are trustees or moral agents (*Khalifah*) representing Allah. Herein lies their identity as Muslims and their sense of dignity since they are special to Allah. But only Muslims have this identity of being Allah's moral agents on earth and so they are also responsible to act on Allah's behalf and destroy those who will not

---

31 Senior research fellow at the Center for the Study of Democracy, University of Westminster. See *The Daily Star,* 9 Feb. 2003, quoted in www.aljazeerah.info. Accessed 20 Oct 2007.
32 See Qur'an Sura 2 on Allah as Creator but note there is no reference to Allah creating Adam in God's Image. Sura 4:1 refers to equality between men and women but again no reference to being created in God's Image. This is supported by an article written by a Muslim woman in *Priscilla Papers,* vol 23:no1, Winter 2009, pp.12–17.
33 Najib Mahfuz, God's World, trans. Akef Abadir and Roger Allen (Minneapolis, Minn.: Bibliotheca Islamica, 1973), p. 3–17.

turn to Him[34] and accept Him as the one and only divine being (Qur'an 5:33,38; 9:5; 45:18).

The worldwide community of Muslims is the primary focus of loyalty. This worldwide community is of great importance.[35] All who confess faith in Allah as the only true God and in the prophethood of Muhammad become part of the Islamic *ummah*. (This is the collective identity of the Muslim people around the world.) This is expressed clearly in the common prayers in the mosques and on the two main festival days — one at the end of the fasting month of Ramadan (*Id-ul-Fitr*) and the other being *Id-ul-Adha*. This sense of a community united in submission to Allah is not only spiritual, but also social and political. It represents both the political as well as the religious dimensions of the community. The annihilation of individuality before Allah allows for the construction of a pillar of Islam, namely, equality of all Muslim people.[36] This equality is uniquely experienced at a Hajj (pilgrimage to Mecca) and gives rise to the intense "spiritual experience" to which Muslim writers who have been on a Hajj refer. The strength of this identification with the *ummah* and the awareness that, worldwide, it is the largest religious community after Christianity is one of the reasons why Muslims have self-confidence in projecting their identity as migrant Muslims in the country in which they have settled.

Thus, the individual is deemed to have worth only in the context of being a member of the *ummah*. Infidels are non-persons.[37] One can see why non-Muslims are the object of hatred: not only because the Qur'an states this, but also because individuals have no special worth before a fellow Muslim or,

---

34   Allah is the Arabic word for God. Philosophically there can be only one God, but the Quranic description of Allah is quite different to the biblical description of God. Also the Qur'an reduces Jesus to being a prophet and miracle worker but will not accept his own declaration that "the Father and I are one" (John 10:30) and thus they also dismiss the cross event and the consequent understanding of God's offer of forgiveness.
35   Maulana Muhammad Ali in *The Religion of Islam*, argues that this unity in Islam "is the greatest civilizing force the world has ever known," p8.
36   For my certainty about this annihilation, I refer to a Muslim writer in Morocco, Fatima Mernissi, *Islam and Democracy: Fear of the Modern World*, trans. by Mary Jo Lakeland (New York, N.Y.: Addison-Wesley, 1992), p. 110. Note also Q2:13–14, which equalises all followers of Islam.
37   Q4:89, 95; 8:12,14–17, 59–60; 9:5, 29,123; 47:4; 5:51, 57.

indeed, before Allah.³⁸ This is further highlighted by the practice of honour killing. A family has honour as a member of the *ummah*, and if one member of the family behaves in a way which is contrary to *Sharia*, or, even worse, against the *Shahada* (the Islamic creed and this means that one is an apostate), then the family has lost its honour before the *ummah*. As the fundamentals of Muslim identity are non-negotiable, the only way forward is to kill the person who has brought dishonour and thus enable the family to regain its honour within the *ummah*.³⁹ A Muslim is unlikely to see past the clear instructions of Muhammad and will not readily reject the collective identity. The Christian's greatest way forward is to pray for Jesus to reveal himself to that person. Then they can develop a new identity in Jesus who they may have met in a dream.

Sikhism self-image

Sikhism developed in reaction to Hinduism and Islam. It places an emphasis on the symbols of identity which every Sikh must have and these symbols strengthen the view that each person matters. The Sikh does believe in the Muslim idea of an ever-present "god" and in the Hindu idea of punishment and rewards reflected in reincarnation. Sikhs are committed to the welfare, equality and freedom of every person as they hope to see an ideal society develop, based on spiritual understanding. Hence they do care for one another — a pattern which developed because they were a minority religious group in a Hindu/Muslim society.⁴⁰ They also recognise the need to establish themselves as a worthwhile and a persistent minority in which each person is valued. The Christian also is committed to the value and importance of each person and this needs to be discussed with a Sikh whenever possible.

---

38   See Bat Ye'or, *Islam and Dhimmitude* (Lancaster, UK: Gazelle Book Services, 2002), for an outline of the reduction of personal status of non-Muslims who agree to pay the tax (*jizya*) so as not to be killed or made a slave; also Q9:29.

39   Maulana Muhammad Ali in *The Religion of Islam* argues that the Qur'an does not require the death of an apostate and quotes the Mecca Q2:256: "there is no compulsion in religion" (p.439). But, the Hadith, which is just as significant as the Qur'an, does declare the need to kill an apostate; see Sahih Bukhari 9.88.6922 and 4.56.3017. There are numerous examples of this penalty being carried out; see Robert Spencer, *The Truth about Muhammad* (Washington, DC: Regnery Publishing, 2006), pp.147ff. Also see my book, David Claydon, *Islam, Human Rights and Public Policy.*

40   Hindus are 74% of the population, Muslims are 14%, Christians are 6% and Sikhs 2%.

Shintoism self-image

This is the traditional religion in Japan and gained its ideas from Buddhism and Confucianism. It is not so much a religion as being essentially the Japanese culture. It has no founder or sacred text. There is an awareness of a remote divine impersonal force in the form of *kami*. Worship involves responding to divine forces and the need to respect one's ancestors. Self-image is linked to being Japanese and behaving in the Japanese way which includes a willingness to participate in Shinto rituals. Failure to participate results in denigrating the person in every possible way including not treating people as people. There is complete loss of human rights. One Christian response is to show that the real *kami* can be known in the living person of Jesus.

Identity movements and their self-image

There are religious and political movements which identify themselves in specific ways and make clear demands on their members. Membership is linked to the desire to be committed to the identity being promoted. For instance, there was the Nazi Party (National Socialists) which promoted the superiority of the Aryan people, the commitment to nationalism, and to a policy which was antagonistic to non-Aryans and to homosexuals as well as deformed people. It thus had no regard for humanity as such and only recognised one brand of humanity. Personal image was grounded in being a member of the Nazi party, otherwise you were a non-person and likely to be placed in a concentration camp, tortured and/or killed.

There are many other identity groups. One example is the "Nation of Islam" in the USA which is led currently by Louis Farrakhan. It holds to the conviction that the black race was supreme in the past and will reign again. Another group is the white supremacist group known as the Ku Klux Klan and it may still have some small groups today. It was a racist movement and it greatly influenced the personal identity of its members. The members may already have been white supremacists, but their membership of this group reinforced their identity. There are other groups which appear from time to time such as the Worldwide Church of God.[41] It is helpful to recognise such groups and the way the identity of members is strengthened by involvement. Scientology may well fall into this category.[42] Reaching a member of an identity group is hard and usually requires personal witness, over a long period of time, to the reality of faith in Christ.

Evil spirits and witches

Cultures in some countries resist a rational view of life and see all that happens as a consequence of the action of evil spirits. For these people the spiritual dimension is an essential part of their identity, which means that a spiritual agency is involved in almost everything they do. These people fear the work of evil and their identity is an outworking of their fears and hopes linked to the challenges of life. A Christian response is to refer to Christ's work on the cross as having a permanent effect and that in Christ we can be protected from our fears and know that the Holy Spirit is at work in our lives. Yet this response would involve a change of identity and such a change requires alternative symbols and values. The vacuum needs to be filled.

Humanism

Whilst humanism is not a religion, it nevertheless replaces religious connections for those who are committed to a humanist world view. The humanist thinks about him/herself in terms of personal dignity and capacity for self-realisation as an autonomous, self-evolving entity. As there is no external basis for one's personal value, it means that personal worth relates to personal achievements, to one's ethnicity and the capacity to think through issues. It assumes that there is no eternal existence of the "person" (the soul for some) and therefore one lives only for the present. Attitudes towards other people are an outworking of one's own value system and world view.

---

41 Founded in 1892 by Herbert W. Armstrong — this group denies the Trinity and hell and sees themselves as the only true church.
42 Founded in 1954 by Ron Hubbard and involves psychoanalysis. It believes that there are many gods in the universe and it denigrates the cross. There is no hell and it embraces reincarnation.

The Christian response is to dialogue with the humanist and indicate that humanity is in itself precious to the God who has revealed himself.

Questions for reflection or discussion

→ To what extent is it helpful to know what others believe?

→ How can knowing this clarify or strengthen our own beliefs?

Chapter 19

Ethnic Identity and the Missionary Challenge

Racism is a misleading ideology; yet race and nationalism show that God is one who loves variety.

The way our inheritance may become localised

A major dimension of our identity is our ethnic inheritance. This, however, never stands on its own. It is always mixed with language, culture, race, religion and nationality. Others tend to determine our identity on our appearance in the first instance. This may be indicative of a particular people group, but such an assessment is superficial. For instance, if I have an African appearance, it really says very little. I could have been born in an African country (and there are 52 of them, with numerous languages, races and religions!), or I could have been born locally. My cultural stance is very likely to be that of the country in which I grew up. Likewise my language is likely to belong to the country of my up-bringing. So if, for instance, I am of African stock, but born in an English-speaking country, English may be my only language. On the other hand, I could be brought up by parents with the home country language and speak the local language as well. This is typical of missionaries whose children speak the local language (often better than their parents!), but in the home speak the language of the country from which their parents came. They like many others grow up bi-lingual.

The word "ethnicity" is a common word in our language. It comes from the Greek (*ethnos*) and is used in the Greek NT to refer to "people-groups", generally the Gentiles. In everyday literature it normally refers to a people-group among whom have been transmitted certain behaviours which have been handed down from generation to generation. This people-group may share a common geography, language, history and possibly religion. It is unlikely that any "ethnic" group shares in the one language or one religion as there are usually a number of languages and/or religions within any apparent ethnic group. So ethnicity may be a cultural indicator and other people can be quickly confused about the identity of someone until they get to know the person, who then reveals something about him/herself. This confusion can lead not only to wrong assumptions, but also to wrong attitudes. So it is out of these wrong attitudes that racism develops.

Racism is a misleading ideology

Racism is a cultural value and becomes an ideology defining for the onlooker certain values and behaviours. This means that the onlooker has dehumanised the other and has removed the concept that all people are created in God's image. This generates unhelpful ideas of inequality which can lead to rejection — and rejection distorts relationships and the real personal identity of the other. Racism has been the cause of massive social problems in our communities and these days is condemned under the laws of non-discrimination. However, this doesn't prevent individuals from thinking wrong thoughts. Racism can be overcome as we get to know the other person through friendship and see beyond what is superficial.

God does see nations and tribes as an expression of variety

The biblical position is that God's creative activity has been diverse. It is part of his pleasure to create with variety, which we recognise as we look at the whole of creation (Psalm 19). Even God's instruction to Abraham is that he will be the father of many nations (Genesis 15:5; 22:17–18, Romans 4:18) and in the book of Revelation we find that people of all tribes and nations will be gathered at the throne of God (7:9–12). On the occasion of the tower of Babel (Genesis 11) God scattered the people by language. He ordained this new form of social relations through nationalism as part of human identity. The beauty of variety is with us and will remain with us until we are joined together in the "new Jerusalem". Notwithstanding the Tower of Babel, God did create the human race as one. We are all descended from Adam and Eve, and so while there are cultural differences, nevertheless there is only one race, the human race which God ordained and created in his image and for his pleasure. May we enjoy his enjoyment!

Missionaries adapt

The missionary dimension of this is that Jesus' gift of salvation is for all people. All have fallen short of the kingdom of God and all who accept Jesus as Lord and Saviour will be redeemed (John 17:20–23; Romans 3:22–23). Missionaries come from many countries. Their status is not limited by race or nationality. They seek to cross boundaries so as to make known the message of salvation and to help Christians to grow in their faith and in its application to daily lives.

Within the missionary world, there is always a concern to find ways of taking the gospel to people-groups which have not heard it. So missionaries may determine groups by a category. One such category is that of ethnic groups living in a country other than the birth country. They are known as a diaspora. Another group with special features could be those who cannot read (known as oral learners). In this way missionaries have a high regard for the identity of each group and the need to let those in each group know about the one who wants them to be in a living eternal relationship with him. Missionaries also train in order to work among an ethnic group so that they will understand the culture and if needed the language and history of each group. When missionaries live in a foreign culture they adapt themselves to the local identity as far as they can, by eating the local food, speaking the local language and often wearing clothes like those worn locally.

The work of the missionary need not take away from the identity of the people among whom they work. Some centuries ago it was considered that missionaries sought to change the culture by "civilising" the locals. There may have been an element of this particularly in the wearing of clothes and sometimes in the style of church buildings, but this has not been so for at least the last hundred years. Missionaries do not seek to change culture, but to enable Christians to apply biblical values to their culture, just as we would apply biblical values to our culture.

> **Missionaries do not seek to change culture but to enable Christians to apply biblical values to their culture**

Diaspora can function in different ways

Diaspora groups often associate in the migrant country. They may do so to nourish their own culture and be able to use their own language. In some cases they will want to reinforce among each other their traditional religion. The religious commitment may require them to wear certain clothes, to eat certain foods and to attend their religious events. Such behaviour can bring about a pattern of self-determined segregation. Some changes are certainly needed if there is to be integration and non-discrimination. In some situations there is a desire by a diaspora group to have their own laws applied, but this is unacceptable as it means that the country will have two or more sets of laws and courts and this creates a major division in society. The division is not just between those members and the rest of society. It exists also because many of the migrants of that group came to the migrant country so as to get away from the legal system perpetuated in their home country, and they want the freedom that the new country allows. Those who migrate from their country of origin may allow their nationalism to dominate the many layers of their personal identity, but these people can become part of the country of their migration while not losing the positive elements of the culture from which they have come.

Questions for reflection or discussion

→ What are some of the characteristics exhibited by "racism"?

→ Suggest ways racism can be overcome.

Chapter 20

The Identity of the Church and Personal Connections

Our Christian identity is reinforced by belonging to the body of Christ, and our church membership can contribute to the nation's understanding of its Christian heritage.

Belonging to the body of Christ

We are incorporated in Jesus Christ as our Lord and Saviour from the moment we believe in the gospel of salvation. This is an act of faith. We have not met Jesus as many people did twenty centuries ago, but we have faith, that Jesus did walk this earth and did die on the cross for us as revealed in the Scriptures, and such faith is confirmed in us as we recognise the leading of the Holy Spirit in our daily lives. Hence we can state as outlined in chapters 12 and 13, that we are "in Christ". This fact is described in the New Testament as being part of the "body of Christ". The image points to our dependence on Christ for our membership in God's kingdom; to the way the different parts of the body come together so that there is a unity which Christians across the world have in Christ; and to our mutual responsibility to pray for and to care for one another. So there is in this picture an awareness that Christians belong together no matter where they live, or who they are.

> *For as in one body we have many members, and the members do not all have the same function, so we,*

> *though many, are one body in Christ, and individually members one of another. (Romans 12:4–5)*
>
> *...there may be no division in the body, but the members may have the same care for one another. If one member suffers, all suffer together; if one member is honoured, all rejoice together. Now you are the body of Christ and individually members of it. (1 Corinthians 12:25–27)*
>
> *There is one body and one Spirit — just as you were called to the one hope that belongs to your call — one Lord, one faith, one baptism, one God and Father of all, who is over all and through all and in all. (Ephesians 4:4–6)*

The gathering of God's people

This body metaphor is one of a number of metaphors describing the church in the NT. Other metaphors for church include being the "bride of Christ" (2 Corinthians 11:2; Ephesians 5:32); God's family (Ephesians 3:14–15); the "flock of God" (1 Peter 5:2); the "household of God" (Ephesians 2:20–22); God's "holy temple" (1 Corinthians 3:16–17); and the foundation of truth (1 Timothy 3:15–16). Obviously, Christ is the "head of the body" as discussed above, but thus it becomes that Christ is the head of the church (Ephesians 1:22; 5:23; Colossians 1:18).

The term used in the NT for "church" (*ecclesia*) indicates an assembly of people called by an authority. In NT days this word was used when the town authorities called the citizens to gather and respond to issues raised. So when Paul uses the term in writing to the early church, he is setting up a gathering which is different from the one in which citizens are called to meet together. He is calling believers in Jesus to gather together. When one of his letters is to be read by all the churches in the country then his opening is, "To the churches of Galatia" (Galatians 1:2); otherwise he writes in the singular form, such as, "To the church of the Thessalonians" (1 Thessalonians 1:1), and "to the church of God that is in Corinth" (1Corinthians 1:1). When Paul writes to Christians in a city who may be scattered and not gathered, he says, "To the saints who are in Ephesus" (Ephesians 1:1).

There are also references in the NT letters indicating that members of the "body of Christ" are already members of the heavenly assembly, to which we all belong even if scattered, and which we will fully realise when we join Christ in heaven:

> *God, being rich in mercy, because of the great love with which he loved us, even when we were dead in our trespasses, made us alive together with Christ — by grace you have been saved — and raised us up with him and seated us with him in the heavenly places in Christ Jesus. (Ephesians 2:4–6; see also Colossians 3:1–4)*

When Christ's followers on earth gather together they are fellow members of one particular community. Such a gathering causes the formation of an institution which God uses to reach out to the world, and the church does this in the power and presence of the Holy Spirit. The church's identity is to be found in the fact that it belongs to Jesus and represents him to the world.

The identity of the church in the community

The fact that there is a church community highlights for each one of us our identity as a member. By implication the church gains its identity from what it (the individual members and the institution) does in the community. The church expresses to the nation the presence of God in the world. It is a witness to God's kingdom and an instrument of that kingdom. Thus the identity of the church in entwined with mission and this includes both proclamation and caring ministries. The church as an institution has its own identity in the community. This identity is determined in part by the history of the church in the nation, by the impact which it has on political and community attitudes, by the social acts it undertakes and by the relevance of the faith proclaimed to others. In nations where the church is not allowed to undertake any public activity or is minimised as an institution, it can still be a source of spiritual and emotional strength to its members. Wherever a government will not allow the institutional church to gather together, Christians are still members of the body of Christ and continue to experience that Christ is in them.

We are connected

Behind all these metaphors is the teaching of the connections we have with God and with one another. Most people have an ongoing desire to connect with others, to be in a relationship. This is due to the fact that we are humans, but it is particularly due to the fact that we are created in the image of God. Hence, we reflect something of the triune nature of God. There is a permanent relationship within the Godhead and God is in a relationship with us. As a member of Christ's church our identity is enhanced by the fact that our own church community cares for us. When we need support other members recognise this and their care of us strengthens our self-image as someone who matters to others. If our church fails in these areas we could challenge the leadership to teach and demonstrate that these are important dimensions of being Christ's church. When we travel and meet up with other Christians it is amazing how quickly relationships develop, because of the known factor that we belong to Jesus.

Through the presence of the church in the world, people may know that the Son of God is alive and that they can relate to him. Some people may wish that Jesus were still walking the earth, but he can be known through the existence of the church — his body! The quality of a relationship with the Son of God should be evidenced through the way the church functions.

Understanding a human-managed institution

The confusion among some about the institutional church arises out of the institution's management. This is clearly human, and human beings are sinful, weak and vulnerable. Some members of the institutional church may desire to see their local church organised in a different way because they cannot see how the institutional

> Both the institutional church and individual Christians should demonstrate to the world that Jesus is alive and we can relate to him

aspects tie up with the biblical account of the church. Whatever confusions may exist, the church is the institution which provides a place for Christians to collectively express their worship of God, to connect with each other, to teach each other and to assist each other in various ministries in society. The institutional church is where Christians can gather and it is the Christians who are the "body of Christ". Thus the church may enable Christians to reinforce their identity as Christians and this strengthening of identity can be very helpful particularly when Christians are a minority in the community.

The Christian heritage

Now here we may have a problem as the institution so often fails to reflect the character of Christ, in failing to show forth the identity of our Lord. Yet, for all the problems, the institutional church through its members (the "body of Christ") does show God's love and care for others as evidenced in the charities, hospitals and education systems which it started in so many countries and which continue today.

Leaders in the church often relate to politicians and the government to convey the values which are best understood in the Christian context. The nation may not always be aware of the Christian heritage which has been transmitted through centuries of action by Christians. There may be occasions when this should be communicated to the public. We can read about the political action of William Wilberforce, John Newton and Thomas Buxton against slavery. One may want to argue that there were Christians who were slave masters, but this observation does not eliminate the action of Christian leaders to fight numerous injustices. The church has, as an organisation, set up institutions around the world for medical care, for education, for development and for micro-enterprise which result so often in reflecting God's love for those in need.

In this way Christians can gain an image as people who help others (regardless of their religious or political stance) and so strengthen the identity both of the church and of Christian individuals.

Our identity shapes our behaviour and our behaviour declares our identity.

Question for reflection or discussion

- → How can we know that we are part of "the body of Christ"?
- → Suggest ways individual Christians can reflect Christ in the community.
- → Suggest ways the church as an institution can play a positive role in society.

Chapter 21

A Final Word

We have been on a journey to discover who we are and what it means to be "in Christ". We have noted the influence that circumstances and other people have on our growing sense of self. We have recognised that each of us is unique and a very special part of God's creation.

We have also noted that our identity may change over the years as we grow up and decide what our values are, who our friends are, and what our world view is. But God's identity is always the same. Faithfulness in his unchanging identity is demonstrated through his forgiveness of our sin, his grace in gifting us and thus enabling us to be his ambassadors on earth, and in his power to create and sustain the world.

No matter what changes come about in our own self-image, we are fashioned in the image of God, and so we can work out how to reflect his righteousness, his concern for creation and his love. He is the God of relationships as is made so clear in the trinitarian fact of Father, Son and Holy Spirit, and there can develop within us the capacity to relate to others with dignity and grace, including our communion with Jesus Christ. We matter to our Creator and indeed we depend on him for being the individuals we are. We are strengthened by Jesus living in us, and by our living in him.

> "Rejoice, rejoice, Christ is in you,
> The hope of glory in your hearts.
> He lives! He lives! His breath is in you,
> Arise a mighty army, we arise."[43]

---

43 From *Rejoice* – Graham Kendrick (c) Thankyou Music Admin. by Crossroad Publishing Used by permission.

Bibliography

Books reflecting on philosophy, psychology and other religions

Ali, Maulana Muhammad. *The Religion of Islam*. (Lahore: Ahmadiyya, 1990).

Brandon, Nathaniel. *Six Pillars of Self-Esteem*. (New York: Bantam Books, 1994).

Breakwell, Glynis M. (ed.) *Social Psychology of Identity and the Self Concept*. (London: Surrey University Press, 1992).

Breger, Louis. *Freud: Darkness in the Midst of Vision*. (New York: John Wily & Sons, 2009). (for his discussion of Sigmund Freud and his use of the term "inner identity")

Brettschneider, Wolf-Dietrich and Rüdiger Hein. *Identity, Sport and Youth Development*. (Champaign.IL: Human Kinetics, 1997) (with discussion about *personal identity* and *social identity*)

Burnett, David. G. *The Spirit of Hinduism*. (Oxford: Monarch Books, 2006).

Clines, D.J.A. *Tyndale Bulletin*. (Cambridge: Tyndale House,1968, pp 53–56). (discussion about the image of God, and comments of René Descartes (1596–1650) with his dictum: "I think therefore I am" (in his *The Principles of Philosophy*, Part 1, Principle VII p. 167))

Covell, Ralph R. *Confucius, the Buddha, and Christ*. (Maryknoll, NY: Orbis Books, 1986).

Fox, Kenneth R. *The Physical Self*. (Champaign.IL: Human Kinetics, 1997).

Fronske Health Centre, in www.nau.edul-fronske June 1999 with an outline of some basic elements of self-esteem.

Fromm, Eric. *Man for Himself*. (London: Continuum, 2003).

Lyon, David. *Karl Marx*. (Berkhamstead UK: Lion, 1979).

Magee, Bryan. *The Story of Philosophy*. (New York: Barnes & Noble, 2006). (for discussion about Thomas Aquinas (1224–74 AD); Aristotle (384–322 BC); Epicurus (341–270 BC); and Plato (428–348 BC))

Mercer, K. in J. Rutherford (ed.) *Identity: Community, Culture, Difference*. (London: Lawrence and Wishart, 1990).

Qur'an (an official translation into English by M.M. Khan and M.T. Al-Hilali).

Russell, Bertrand. *Mysticism and Logic.* (New York: Longmans, 1918).

Sampson, E. E. in J. Shotter and KJ Gergen (eds) *Texts of Identity.* (London: Sage, 1989.) (for discussion of the postmodernist position of "self deconstruction")

Wiggins, David. *Identity and Spatio-Temporal Continuity.* (Oxford: Basil Blackwell, 1971).

Williams, D. *Castrating Culture: A Christian Perspective on Ethnic Identity from the Margins.* (Cumbria, UK: Paternoster Press, 2001). (for a discussion about personal identity and the Aboriginal people)

Yen, Chan M. Sheng. *Orthodox Chinese Buddhism.* (New York: Dharma Drum, 2007).

Books reflecting on the Image of God

Berkouwer, G.C. *Man: The Image of God.* (Grand Rapids MI: William B. Eerdmans, 1962).

Bethage, Eberhard. *Dietrich Bonhoeffer: Letters and Papers from Prison.* (London: SCM, 1953).

Cromhout, Markus. *Jesus and Identity.* (Eugene OR: Cascade books, 2007).

Grenz, J. Stanley. *The Social God and the Relational Self.* (Louisville: Westminster John Knox Press, 2001)

————. *The Named God and Question of Being.* (Louisville: Westminster John Knox Press, 2005).

Gruenlar, Royce Gordon. *The Trinity in the Gospel of John.* (Eugene, OR: Wipf & Stock, 2004).

Hill, Edmund. *Being Human.* (London: Geoffrey Chapman, 1984).

La Due, William J. *The Trinity Guide to the Trinity.* (Harrisburg, PN: Trinity Press, 2003).

Lints, Richard, Michael S. Horton, Mark R. Talbot (eds). *Personal Identity in Theological Perspective.* (Grand Rapids MI: William B. Eerdmans, 2006).

Hughes, Philip Edgcumbe. *The True Image: The Origin and Destiny of Man in Christ.* (Grand Rapids MI: William B. Eerdmans, 1989).

Jewett, K. Paul. *Who We Are: Our Dignity as Human.* (Grand Rapids MI: William B. Eerdmans, 1996).

Meehl, Paul, et al. (Symposium). *What, Then, Is Man?* (Saint Louis, MS: Concordia, 1958).

Tournier, Paul. *The Meaning of Persons.* (London: SCM Press, 1976).

Wolterstorff, Nicholas. *Until Justice and Peace Embrace.* (Grand Rapids MI: William B. Eerdmans, 1983).

Books you may be interested in reading which relate to some of the themes in this book

By David Claydon

Connecting across Cultures. Sharing the gospel across cultural and religious boundaries (Melbourne: Acorn Press, 2000).

Islam, Human Rights and Public Policy. (Melbourne: Acorn Press, 2000).

A New Vision, a New Heart, a Renewed Call. Papers from the Lausanne Conference in Thailand, 2004. 3 vols as editor (Carey Library, 2005).

By Robyn Claydon

Doors Are for Walking Through. (Adelaide: SPCKA, 1998).

Keep Walking. (Adelaide: SPCKA, 2001).

One Step at a Time. (Melbourne: Acorn Press, 2010).

By Cecily Paterson

Never Alone. A biography of David and Robyn Claydon (Adelaide: SPCKA, 2006).

www.ingramcontent.com/pod-product-compliance
Lightning Source LLC
Chambersburg PA
CBHW022017290426
44109CB00015B/1205